The Voices of Angels

In October 1999, Francesca Brown was diagnosed with ME and virtually bedridden for two years. However, in 2001 an angel appeared to her and helped to heal her illness. She made a full recovery and Francesca has been in daily contact with the angels ever since, and she continues to work with them as a conduit to those in need. She lives in Ireland and is married with two children. She is the author of *My Whispering Angels* (Hachette Books Ireland, 2009). *The Voices of Angels* is her second book.

Contact Francesca at francesca.brown1@gmail.com
or on Twitter @angelfran.

www.irishministryofangels.com

THE VOICES OF ANGELS

*Inspirational Stories and Divine Messages from
Ireland's Angel Whisperer*

HACHETTE
BOOKS
IRELAND

First published in 2011 by Hachette Books Ireland
First published in paperback in 2012 by Hachette Books Ireland

Copyright © 2011 Francesca Brown

1

A CIP catalogue record for this title is available from the British Library.

ISBN 978 1 444 72537 7

Typeset in AGaramond 13/21pt and Roelandt BT.
by Bookends Publishing Services.

Printed and bound in Great Britain by CPI Group (UK) Ltd, Croydon, CR0 4YY

Hachette Books Ireland policy is to use papers that are natural, renewable
and recyclable products and made from wood grown in sustainable forests.
The logging and manufacturing processes are expected to conform to the
environmental regulations of the country of origin.

Hachette Books Ireland
8 Castlecourt Centre
Castleknock
Dublin 15, Ireland

A division of Hachette UK Ltd
338 Euston Road
London NW1 3BH
www.hachette.ie

To my two wonderful sons, Jason and Dwayne
for all their love and support.

For reasons of privacy and to protect identities, names and identifying details have been changed throughout.

Acknowledgements

I WOULD LIKE TO THANK THE STAFF OF HACHETTE Books Ireland for all their help and belief in me and the angels. Special thanks to Breda Purdue, MD, my editor Ciara Considine, and to Joanna, Ruth and Bernard for all their help and kindness.

I would also like to thank Ciara Foley and Fenella Bates of Hodder & Stoughton, Claire from PR and Peter McNulty.

I would like to take this opportunity to thank the O'Sullivan family from Shannon, County Clare. It is said that people come into our lives for a reason, and this is true. Thank you Don and Joanne for all your help and support. To Liam (Grandad) and Mary (Granny) for their friendship and kindness. To Joanne and Cathy for help with typing.

To a gifted lady, June Considine, for her help and guidance in putting this book together. Thank you.

I want to thank my beautiful team of angels and spirit guides who have inspired me to write this book. They have never let me down. I have been blessed to have them in my life. A special acknowledgement to the many people that I have met on my journey. Their kindness is astonishing and I appreciate their willingness to be always ready to help and support me.

I especially want to thank Fran. He is the love of my life and has always been there for me to understand my journey and support me every step of the way.

I am truly blessed.

Francesca
June 2011

Contents

Whispers

Deep in the centre of my being
I hear a voice
That lives deeply within me.
This voice is reaching out
Beyond a world of light
To touch the heart of everything
That lies within me.

It speaks softly so I may hear
The truth of love.
So that I may come to know
And to understand
That when I stand in this light
I will know my way home.

By Angel Jonathan
Channelled by Francesca Brown

Prologue

TEN YEARS AGO, I WAS TOUCHED BY AN ANGEL and my world changed forever. I described that amazing journey in *My Whispering Angels*. Now, in *The Voices of Angels*, I hope you will return with me once again into that wondrous realm. I want to share with you the sights I have witnessed, the blessings I have received and the struggles that, sometimes, caused my footsteps to falter. But throughout every stage of this astonishing journey, I have been supported by the many angels who have revealed themselves to me.

I want you to hear their voices, feel their presence, understand the unconditional love that they offer you. I have included simple visualisation and meditation exercises to help you open channels of communication with your angels, along with powerful affirmations that have been channelled to me by my special guide, Angel Ann.

Through my intercession with Angel Ann, many pathways have opened up to me. Through her support, I have found myself communicating more and more with those spiritual souls who have passed into the world of light. They come to me with messages of comfort that I can bring to their loved ones who wait behind. I sense their presence in a profound way and am always humbled when I speak for them.

In the two wonderful years that have followed the publication of my first book, I have been invited to travel the length and breadth of Ireland to bring a deeper understanding of the power of angels to people. During all of this travelling, I have been accompanied by my husband Fran, who was once told by his angel that he would be my constant support. And this, indeed, has proved to be the case. I have given angel readings and workshops where people came to experience the power and simplicity of their own angels. I've also held angel evenings, where I interacted with a live audience. Many leave at the end of these evenings with comfort in their hearts and an understanding that our spirits live on long after we depart our earthly world.

Angels are part of everything that is within us. They are the keepers of our souls, the keepers of our light. They are the voices within us, the spiritual beam that opens our hearts and minds to the amazing world around us. They do not live our lives for us, but they are there at all times to give us the advice we need, along with their compassion and empathy.

They teach us that we are worthy of all that is within us and they help us to look upon our lives as a precious gift. To know an angel is to know God, and they will be there in their splendour to take us back once again into a world of light when God eventually welcomes us home.

Those gentle, beautiful spirits of light exist far beyond our worldly cares – but they know us better than we know ourselves. They motivate and encourage us to be the best at whatever we choose to do. They do not judge us for the mistakes we make but help us to believe that no matter what challenges we face, they will always support us. They help us to understand that we all have a purpose to our lives. Even in times of negativity and unhappiness, change is always possible if we have the courage to seek it, and to ask for their help.

Angels have been my mentors, as well as my friends, but my journey with them might never have happened. There was a time when I smiled at the idea that such heavenly beings actually existed – or that they could influence the pattern of our lives. I listened politely to people, including my own sister Elaine, who expressed their own belief in angels and their understanding of this spiritual realm. I dismissed such stories, despite the fact that within my own life, some extraordinary manifestations had occurred when I was younger. Now, when I look back, I wonder how I could have been oblivious to their presence. Were my ears blocked to the sound of their voices calling out to me? Was the pace of my mind so fast that I was unable to stop and think, my eyes so blind I could not see their glory surrounding me? But that was ten years ago, a time when I was blissfully unaware that my life was about to change utterly.

1
The Wind of Change

A strong wind blows and carries the voices of angels.
They will cocoon me and show me the next step on my way.
They will encourage me to look beyond
anything I have ever known.
My heart opens, like a butterfly, to their words.

WHEN MY JOURNEY WITH THE ANGELS BEGAN, I was a home-maker and mother. I loved power-walking and other energetic activities. I enjoyed being outdoors, the feel of the wind against my skin, my mind and body working in harmony as the miles built up and my thoughts slowed down until all my concentration was focused on the road ahead. I played squash with my friends and enjoyed regular games of pitch and putt. Overall, I was active, engaged and in control of my health.

I was an ordinary housewife leading an ordinary life until, suddenly, my energy began to slip away. I became tired all the time. When I visited friends for dinner, I fell asleep before the meal was over and Fran, my husband, had to take me home. I got up in the morning and wanted to go back to bed within an hour. The simple household chores that I normally did without even thinking about them were beyond me. I could no longer take part in any of the family activities that I had always enjoyed with Fran and my teenage sons, Jason and Dwayne. At the time, Fran was working as a taxi driver. When he returned home from a shift, he had to overcome his own tiredness and cook for himself and our sons. When the boys returned from school in the late afternoon, I was usually in bed or resting on the sofa, unable to do anything other than greet them. My muscles, particularly the muscles in my legs, ached with an unbearable intensity whenever I tried to move.

I tried to cope, not to give way to depression. For the first time, my body had taken over my mind – despite my keep-fit regimes and the energy I had always relied on to bring me through each busy day, it had betrayed me. I attended specialists and they carried out numerous medical tests. Each one came back negative, including one for multiple sclerosis, which my doctor was ninety-nine per cent convinced would be positive.

I lay in bed all day, raging against this overwhelming lethargy, the feeling that my body had become a dead weight. On one hand, I was relieved that my tests were negative but they added to my worry that my illness would never be diagnosed, never cured.

My doctor suggested I was suffering from stress. What stress? Until this happened, I had been content with my life. I had a warm circle of friends and an active social life. I had had the occasional ups and downs, like everyone else, but there was nothing I couldn't handle, nothing that should bring about the exhaustion that was practically turning me into a bed-bound invalid. My life was closing down around me and I was helpless to prevent it happening.

In the end, after much investigation, I was diagnosed with myalgic encephalomyelitis (better known as ME or Chronic Fatigue Syndrome). I had little knowledge of the disease and expected my specialist to prescribe medication to treat the condition. I was in despair when he told me there was no known treatment. He was unable to put a time limit on my illness, but believed it could take as long as seven years before I showed signs of recovery.

This was the lowest point in my life. I was trapped within the four walls of my bedroom and the memories of happier times with my family seemed to belong to another era. Little did I realise that this sad episode would foreshadow a new life, one that would open my heart and my mind to the presence of angels and their wonderful, restorative powers of healing.

Since that time, I've travelled a long and astonishing journey with the angels, but in those days, alone and confined to my bed, I thought I was going crazy when, one afternoon, an extraordinary manifestation took place before my eyes. The atmosphere in the room began to change. I didn't understand what was happening and simply assumed I was drifting off to sleep. But my eyes were open and so I figured I was day dreaming when human figures, men and women, gradually appeared in front of me. They seemed to emerge from a haze and, as they became more clearly defined, I could make out their features and the clothes they were wearing. I recognised the long, ruffled skirts worn by the women as a style from the Victorian era. Their elegant jackets emphasised their tiny waists and some of them wore bonnets. All the men wore high hats and fitted jackets. I was convinced my imagination was working overtime – I couldn't think what else it could be. I blinked hard, convinced they would have disappeared when I reopened my eyes. Instead, I was able to see them more clearly, although they appeared to be oblivious to me and their surroundings. My own surroundings seemed to dissolve, and it was as if I was suspended between two worlds. They walked up and down my bedroom in an unhurried way and never once glanced in my direction. My rational mind refused to accept the evidence of my eyes. I hoped desperately that I was dreaming, one of those dreams which you recognise as a dream yet you are unable to wake from it. The only alternative was that I was going crazy.

I was not on any medication so this was not a hallucinatory reaction to drugs. I was terrified yet compelled to watch, afraid to move in case I drew their attention to me. I had no idea how long this manifestation lasted, but gradually it faded and I once again became aware of my surroundings. I was still sitting up in bed, wide awake and mesmerised. I did not mention what had happened to my family. I could imagine their disbelief and Fran's concern that my illness was finally affecting my mind.

The figures returned the following day and the day after that. On the third day, a man in a black coat stopped by my bed, looked straight at me and said, 'You're not going to lie there for the rest of your life, are you?'

My terror increased. Now I was hearing voices. On another occasion, a second man with a grey beard and dressed in working clothes stopped and said, 'Is it really that bad?' He smiled and walked on past me.

I finally confided in Fran. He was sure I was hallucinating and, as I had guessed, this added greatly to his worry about my condition. Around the same time, my doctor, who knew nothing about these manifestations, suggested that I go to a support group that met once a week in the hospital I attended. He believed it would be good for me to mix with other patients, especially as some of them also suffered with ME. Fran managed to help me to the hospital, where I met the group of patients. We formed a circle and our group leader, who was a psychologist, asked us to introduce ourselves. I smiled at a young girl sitting opposite me and, as I did so, the words 'Her father is an alcoholic' flashed into my mind. It seemed as if a voice had just spoken into my ear.

At that same moment, the girl introduced herself and, as she elaborated on her personal life, I was astonished to discover that her father was indeed an alcoholic. While I was trying to adjust to this information, I noticed colours beginning to form around each person in the circle. Some were a dull grey or brown and they clung to people's heads and shoulders. Others were bright red, blue and gold and seemed to spark off each individual's body. When the session ended, and Fran had settled me back into the car, I began to weep. Now, more than ever, I believed I was losing my mind.

Those figures from another era never manifested again but, shortly afterwards, on one unforgettable day, I heard the voice of an angel for the first time. I was lying in my bed, feeling particularly drained and exhausted, when I became aware of a pale blue mist forming before me. I heard a voice, clear as a bell, telling me not to be frightened.

'I'm here to help you,' the voice said.

'Who are you?' I asked.

'I'm a healing angel,' was the reply. 'I'm going to help you to get better.'

'But you don't look like an angel,' I told this apparition. From my childhood, I had carried an image of angels in my mind. They had human features, magnificent wings and radiated a golden light. Was it possible that this pale-blue light was really a divine messenger? Instinctively, I believed she was. My fear disappeared. I listened intently to her words. I must have faith in my recovery, she said. I would get better. As her wondrous blue energy faded, I was filled with hope. I trusted the words she had uttered and longed for her to return.

About a week passed before she appeared again. As I watched and welcomed her divine presence, the blue light transformed into an angel figure that I could identity with my childhood beliefs. She was tall, I guess about six feet in height, and she had a pair of glorious wings. She stood at the foot of my bed and radiated an exquisite energy. I felt ecstatic as I stared at her and knew that I was witnessing something far beyond my understanding. She advised me to start eating certain foods that would aid my recovery. These included honey, kiwi fruit, raisins and currants. I must stop eating white bread because my yeast intake was adding to my health problems.

Fran was mystified when I sent him off with a different shopping list to the usual one. He bought the required foods and I added them to my meals. I began to eat wholemeal bread, even though I had never liked it, and upped my intake of water. I had to leave out potatoes and red meat, but that was not difficult because my appetite had also suffered and I had mainly been existing on bowls of soup.

When my angel appeared again, it was late one evening. She performed a healing ritual, moving her wing to my forehead, my throat and just above my stomach. Each place she indicated to me seemed to come alive with energy.

'These are your energy centres,' she said and advised me to bring my attention to them as often as I could.

In my first book, *My Whispering Angels*, I describe this extraordinary healing process in detail and the amazing journey that followed with this wondrous angel, whom I call Angel Ann.

In time, she advised me to leave my bed and walk to my front gate. What she was suggesting seemed impossible. I had not been downstairs unaided for months. But my trust in her was so great that I decided to try. Fran supported me and we completed the journey together. He continued to help me to take those difficult steps every day and go a little bit farther. Each time I completed this journey, I felt stronger and more positive that I would get my health back.

Then, one joyous day, I was able to walk alone. Nearly eighteen months had passed since I had first been diagnosed with ME. Finally, I could see a new future opening up for me. Little did I realise that this was only the beginning of a transformation that was to change the path of my life forever, and in ways I could never have imagined.

Looking back I can trace a pattern that formed long before I heard the voices of angels. It goes right back to my childhood when, in the innocence of those days, I sought to understand the mystery of a loving and compassionate God.

2

First Confession

My child, many times you have journeyed with me.
Each time I took you to an understanding of who you are.
But you turned in a direction that took you away from me.
You felt lost and alone. Yet your life was always filled with
the essence of my love and light. Still you walked away,
dismissing those feelings that were stirring within you.
The voice of *Who Am I?*

MY MOTHER, ALICE GIBBS, GAVE BIRTH TO ME IN the Rotunda Hospital in Dublin on 19 October 1958. I was christened Penelope and grew up in Finglas on the northside of Dublin. John, my father, worked as a bus driver and we belonged to a working-class community, close-knit and always looking out for each other.

My childhood memories are happy ones. In those days, Finglas still bore the hallmarks of a country village and I remember the freedom of fields and rivers, shady woodlands and long summer evenings at play with my brothers, Michael and Mark, and my sisters, Elaine and Jackie. We lived close to the Tolka River and this flow of water gave us endless hours of fun. We bought fishing rods in the local shops and filled our jars with pinkeens. Once we were released from school, we made a beeline for the fields. We ran, we played, skipped and danced, and believed those days would never end. When we discovered an orchard, we did what all kids do when they come upon a treasure – we filled our jumpers with apples. Needless to say, we were chased by the irate owner but this only made the adventure all the more exciting. Unfortunately, by the time we reached the safety of the lane, most of our forbidden fruit had fallen from our jumpers to the ground.

I was seven years old when I made my First Communion. I enjoyed the fuss over my Communion dress and the shopping trips to buy all the accessories to go with it. When the day arrived, I visited my relations. They gave me presents and money, and, for that one special day, all their attention was fixed on me. Most of all, I longed for the ultimate reward, the receiving of the sacrament of Communion.

But before I could do that, I had to make my First Confession. In school, we practised the routine of entering the confession box. One word seemed to be on everyone's lips. Sin. Our teacher talked a lot about the need to confess our sins; so did my parents, and anyone else who knew what was going to take place within the next few days. This puzzled me.

From what I could gather, when the big day arrived and the priest gave me penance and absolution, I would be in a state of grace, cleansed of all my sins. Then, and only then, could I receive the blessed sacrament into my soul.

I became increasingly upset over the idea of telling a priest that I had committed sins. How could I, a small child of seven, have sins to confess? We were all children of a loving God. So we had been taught. So how could my soul be black from the weight of all my wrongdoings? This question kept bothering me, even as I was drawn along in the inevitable direction of the confession box.

I remember sitting in the church with my classmates. We were serious, scared and silent as, one by one, we entered the confessional. The questions were still going round in my head when my turn came. Inside the confessional, a red light was shining. As soon as I knelt down, a little hatch was pulled across. A deep voice asked me to confess my sins. I recognised the priest from Sunday mass. The sight of this familiar face helped me to gather my courage. He would understand my confusion.

'I've no sins, Father,' I said. 'I'm only a little girl. How can I have any sins?'

Without waiting for a reply, I hurried from the confession box and returned to my seat. I heard a door opening and, looking over my shoulder, I realised that the priest had followed me. He did not look particularly pleased as he approached my teacher. They had a short conversation, their eyes fixed on me the whole time. I was frightened but defiant, still prepared to argue my case. The priest returned to the confessional to continue his duties and my teacher sat beside me. She was a gentle person and I was very fond of her. She looked at me strangely and explained that I must confess my sins. She said we were all sinners and that it was important that my soul was cleansed for my First Holy Communion. After a lot of persuasion, I finally agreed to confess something bad. I thought back to a row I'd had with Patricia, my best friend. I'd called her a 'bitch'. I knew this was a word that should never be used under any circumstances and so it seemed to fit into the category of 'Sin'.

'Halleluiah,' said my teacher. 'At last we have a sin.'

So back I went, armed with my sin, and confessed it. My penance was three Our Fathers and three Hail Marys. I had to ask God's forgiveness and promise never to repeat that word again, or do anything else that would offend God. I've often wondered if God felt I dishonoured Him by trying to refuse the grace of absolution – or did He understand my instinctive belief that He was an embracing, loving deity who saw the goodness and the purity of children, rather than their misdeeds.

A few days later, I made my First Communion. This was joyful and celebratory. I felt grown-up and thrilled that I would receive this sacrament every time I went to mass.

My memory of those two occasions, and my contrasting reactions to them, has always remained with me. Memories can stay with us for a reason, and it is only later in life, when we can articulate the confusions of our childhoods, that we understand the part they played in our development. With the hindsight of all that has happened to me since, I wonder if I was being prepared, at some childish, subconscious level, for the visitation of my angels and the beliefs I hold today.

While I argued about the rights and wrongs of the confessional, I never doubted the presence of angels. I grew up believing in my guardian angel, but without understanding the true nature of her existence.

The Catholic Church in which I was raised was quite strict, and it was considered wrong to question your faith. My parents followed the dictates of their Church by attending mass on Sundays, but their attitude to religion was relaxed. At home, a love of God was not drilled into us through a fear of damnation – but that approach was instilled into us in school. The catechism we learned had little in it about love and compassion. Instead of leading me to God as I grew older, it led me farther away from Him. I did not appreciate or understand – as I do today – that He lived within me. Instead, I saw Him as a stern authority figure, a separate entity who was observing my sins from some distant sphere. If I questioned this approach or tried to understand the mystery of my religion, I was accused of dishonouring my faith. Instead of my childhood curiosity being recognised as a desire to grow closer to God, I was reprimanded, and told that I must not question the workings of the Divine Ordinance.

I attended Sunday mass and coped as best I could with the boredom of a long-drawn-out service. The prayers and the ritual did not bring me closer to God. I no longer wanted to know Him. My thoughts were elsewhere as I waited for an appropriate moment to slip from the Church. I was confused and drifting farther away from my faith yet, somehow, deep within me, I knew I had to find Him in my own way. But it would take me many years and a long painful journey to discover the answer to my questions – and to understand the true significance of God and the angels in my life.

3

Awakening to Angels

*As we journey onwards with our spirit, we find a connection
to the many things around us. Our spirit contains our lives,
our purpose and our journey on this earth.
When we merge with the spirit and believe that a source
stands with us, we will achieve great things.
We will not doubt ourselves. We will be confident and strong.
We will have no fear for we know in our hearts that
we are beautiful human beings with the capability to change.*

ON THE AFTERNOON THAT THE PEOPLE FROM
another era moved around my bedroom, I had absolutely no
idea what was happening. My fear that I was having a nervous
breakdown was very real. All the elements were there: my
lack of energy, the dread that I would not get better for years,
if ever, my sense of helplessness and a belief that my life no
longer counted for anything. I struggled constantly against
severe depression and there were days when all I wanted to

do was pull the duvet over my head to shut out the world. But even if I had done so, my visitors would have made their presence known to me. Such manifestations, as I would later discover, are no respecters of walls, duvets or the subconscious mind.

I now understand that I was witnessing my first glimpse into the psychic realm. This phenomena is often a comfort to people who have just lost a loved one. It is not uncommon for them to actually feel such a presence around them for some time after he or she has passed on, and there can be occasional sightings of the departed person, or some other significant but mystifying sign that does not connect to our rational way of thinking. Over the years, I have come to know and understand this realm intimately and how to work within its sphere in a positive way.

As I gradually grew stronger, with the encouragement of my healing angel, I walked a little farther every day and experienced the intense joy of being back on my feet. I settled back again into a normal routine. Simple family activities that I had taken for granted until I could no longer participate in them gave me the greatest joy. But, of course, my life was never going to be normal again, at least not in a way that it had been.

I was still in communication with Angel Ann, who was now materialising several times a week. Gradually, my fears disappeared, as did any lingering doubts about the existence of the angels. I realised I was embarking on an amazing spiritual journey and I was open to Angel Ann's guidance. I could see her clearly each time she came and I loved to look at her; so tall and sleek with her beautiful wings open wide. I spoke internally to her and her voice was soft and reassuring when she answered me. She taught me how to channel. At first, I had no idea what she meant by this, but she explained that I must be able to connect with the realm of angels and the spirit world whenever it was necessary. This concept was so astonishing to me and I felt overwhelmed by such responsibility. Opening myself to the presence of angels had been an intense and fulfilling experience, but everything had happened so fast that I felt as if I was being buffeted by these psychic encounters. Angel Ann's manifestations were wonderful, but afterwards I found it difficult to return to the reality of my everyday life. I needed to be grounded and in control of these remarkable occurrences.

I learned two important exercises that benefitted me during these early days: grounding and releasing. By practising these exercises on a daily basis, I was able to look at different areas of my life where I needed help. One such area was a fear that I was not worthy to communicate with the realm of angels. Perhaps the voices I was hearing were not those of angels but were manifested by my own imagination. I was being asked to take an enormous step from my own world where there are rational explanations for everything. In accepting this world of spirit and mystery, I had to abandon everything I had been conditioned to believe. I could embrace this new experience with absolute faith – or use my free will and walk away.

I did not want to walk away. My mind yearned to embrace everything that was opening before me, and those periods of deep meditation centred my mind. Angel Ann taught me the importance of releasing any emotional, physical or mental blocks that could prevent me hearing her voice and the voices of angels who came to help me with specific information.

As my life began to change, I grew anxious for the company of people who would understand what I was experiencing. I joined a meditation class where we discussed channelling and its impact on our work. Suddenly, in the middle of a discussion, I felt compelled to lean towards the woman sitting opposite me and ask her if she had a brother called Eamon. When she said she did, I gave her a short, precise message about an illness that was affecting him. She was surprised that I should have such personal information but agreed that what I had told her was correct. I had heard the voice of Angel Ann relaying this information quite distinctly to me. The leader of the meditation group seemed surprised by the preciseness of the message and asked how long I had been open to channelling such knowledge from the angels.

'Only a few months,' I replied. I explained about my illness and how the intervention of the angels had brought about my recovery.

'That can't be true,' the group leader interjected. 'You couldn't receive a message like that in such a short time. It took years before I was able to interpret that kind of information.'

This woman's disbelief stung me. I wanted to sink back into myself and become invisible. Effectively, although not in so many words, she had accused me of deceiving the group. When we are on the edge of something new and powerful in our lives, we are like fragile buds about to open and our confidence is easily crushed. Constructive criticism is helpful but negativity can be detrimental. The woman had been a good teacher but her ego was dominant and I knew by her reaction that she would undermine my confidence. However, before I left the class, another woman spoke to me.

'I have been travelling this road for sixteen years,' she said. 'Don't throw in the towel at this early stage.' It was good advice and I accepted it. But I never returned to that particular group.

As my senses sharpened, so did my conviction that my life was being guided by angels and that I needed to heed their advice. One particular memory has always remained with me. I had planned to meet my friends one morning for coffee. I sat into the driver's seat of my car and turned on the engine. As I was about to put the car into reverse gear, I heard a voice in my head. The words were quite distinct. 'You forgot your perfume.'

Perfume is my weakness. I love using it and always feel half-dressed when I forget to spray it on. I was rushing on this occasion and was about to ignore such a trivial reminder when something quietened my mind. I turned off the engine, intending to return to the house and dab some perfume on my wrists. As the sound of the engine died, I heard another voice. This voice was high-pitched and most definitely earth-bound. It also sounded very frightened. I realised it belonged to a child. Horrified, I got out of the car and followed it. A little boy, about three years of age, who lived across the road from my house, had crawled under the boot of the car. He had been terrified by the noise of the engine and was crouched into a tight ball, afraid to move. Without doubt, I would have run over him if I had not been stopped in my tracks by Angel Ann appealing directly to my vanity.

I lifted him in my arms and began to cry as I imagined what could have happened if I had reversed down my driveway. I carried him back to his own house. Workmen were doing renovation work to the house and had left the front door open. His mother hadn't known that he had escaped.

'From now on, never doubt the presence of angels in our lives,' I told her after I had explained what had happened. She too was deeply emotional when she realised how narrowly her child had avoided a tragic accident that would have marked us both for the rest of our lives.

As the years passed, my trust in my angels grew even stronger. The direction of my life was becoming clearer all the time. Word spread among my friends and neighbours that I was in communication with angels. I was asked to do angel readings. People came to my house to see if I could communicate with their loved ones who had passed on or, at a personal level, if I could link into the blockages in their own lives that were preventing them from moving on.

Initially, I was nervous of exposing myself to the scrutiny of others. I knew their expectations would be great, but I knew I had no magic wand to wave that would banish their problems. I was also unsure if I could interpret correctly the messages that came to me from the spirit world. To hear such voices and believe what they told me meant taking an incredible leap of faith. Yet Angel Ann was insistent that I was ready to communicate the guidance and advice that people sought. And there were signs – some small, some more significant – that the angels were continuing to work on my behalf.

One of my earliest angel reading sessions involved a group of women who came to see me together. On the day they were due to arrive, I kept smelling fish. It was a fresh ocean smell, pungent yet not unpleasant, but I had no idea where it was coming from. Fish was not on my dinner menu, nor had I any in my fridge or freezer. Yet the smell persisted. When the first woman entered the room the smell grew stronger. She was beautifully dressed and made-up. Her perfume was a subtle, delicate fragrance yet it could not dispel the odour in the room. I was uneasy about mentioning this to her in case she thought I was accusing her of smelling of fish. I did not need Angel Ann to tell me that this would be a risky way to open a spiritual dialogue – yet her angel voice urged me to mention it.

Eventually, I took a deep breath and said, 'I'm only beginning to do angel readings so it's possible that I've misinterpreted something. But have you anything to do with fish?'

To my relief, she began to laugh and told me that she ran a fish shop with her husband. Instantly, once this was confirmed, the smell disappeared. I realised this was Angel Ann's way of showing me that I had to trust my psychic awareness. It was an important lesson and one I valued as my reputation spread.

Each step I took was carefully monitored by Angel Ann. She advised me to keep a diary and record how each reading went. If it went well I would write 'W.W.' at the end of each entry. Whenever I began to have doubts she would advise me to check my diary, where practically every reading was marked 'W.W.'.

I was impatient, always anxious to move on to the next level of awareness. But Angel Ann cautioned me not to run before I could walk.

'There is a time for everything,' she would say. 'When that time is right, the information will become clear to you.' She still gives me the same advice to this very day.

On one occasion, I was contacted by a woman who ran a spiritual centre. She invited me to speak about my angels at one of her gatherings. I willingly agreed, but Angel Ann advised me to cancel the arrangement.

'You are not ready yet to do what this woman will ask of you,' she said. Her voice was insistent, but I ignored her advice. What could go wrong? I argued as I headed off to the meeting. All I had to do was to speak about my angels and read some of my poems.

I had started to write poetry. These poems were inspired by the angels and were generally written after I had been in communication with young people who, sadly, had died and passed into the world of light. These poems had a special resonance for the parents and siblings who were left behind.

I ignored the advice from my angel and headed off to meet this group. After I had spoken, the leader of the group asked me to give messages from the spirit world to the people who were present. Basically, what she was asking me to do is what is known as 'platform work', where a psychic stands before a live audience and passes on messages of comfort from their loved ones who have died. I did hope one day to develop my skills and address such an audience, but I had not yet reached that level of competency. I was used to speaking to people on a one-to-one basis and when I received a spirit message, it was carried on the energy we created through our personal link.

I could have refused this woman's request but my ego intervened and I tried to deliver messages to those present.

I did manage to link strongly into one young soul who was anxious to contact his parents. They were deeply moved by the information I relayed to them, but this was a new experience for me and I felt that my line of communication was weak. In some instances, I was unable to hear the voice of Angel Ann. This was my first experience of being unable to communicate with her, and her silence was unnerving. I was aware of the disappointment of some of the people present, but there was nothing I could do about it. On my way home, I asked Angel Ann why she had let me down.

'You did not listen to my voice,' she replied. 'You had to learn by experience that knowledge only comes when you are ready to absorb it.'

Ego and pride, I was discovering, have no place in the angel realm. It was an embarrassing lesson to learn, but it increased my determination to trust the guidance of my angels.

Through meditation, visualisation and other simple exercises that helped to focus my mind, I continued to gain self-assurance. My sons, still teenagers, were, understandably, rather confused by the path I had chosen to travel. It was so outside their normal experience. First they had had to cope with my illness and stand helplessly by as I became a bed-bound invalid, now they had to cope with people calling to our house at all hours, reading features about 'the angel woman' in the local newspapers and my constant reminders that angels were now an essential part of our lives. No wonder they were mystified – and also a little embarrassed. But when it suited them, they were quite happy to call on Angel Ann's intervention.

On one occasion, Dwayne arrived home from school and told me he had to write a poem about the Sellafield nuclear reprocessing plant in Cumbria. After struggling with the Muse for a while and receiving no inspiration, he asked me to ask Angel Ann to write it for him.

'Ask your own angel,' I retorted. 'She'll help you out.'

But Dwayne had no intention of going that far. It was Angel Ann or nothing. Under her guidance, I wrote the poem and he headed off to school with it the following day.

When Dwayne read it out in class his teacher said, 'I don't believe you wrote that poem yourself.'

Dwayne confessed that I had written it.

'Is she a bit of a poet then?' his teacher asked.

'She is,' Dwayne said. 'She loves writing poetry.'

'Why didn't you tell him your poem was written by an angel?' I demanded when he told me about his teacher's reaction.

He looked at me in astonishment and said, 'You must be joking if you think I was going to stand up in front of my classmates and tell them my poem was written by an angel.'

Such an admission would have strained the credulity of most teenagers, so I fully understood his reasons for wanting to keep my angels a secret. However, that was before he discovered that his friends' mothers and sisters were coming to me for angel readings. One evening, after playing a game of football with some local lads, he was staying over in his friend's house when he overheard a conversation between the boy's mother and her friends, who had dropped in for a chat. They were discussing a local psychic who had carried out angel readings for them. They were astonished over the accuracy of the readings and the insights they had gained into their lives. As the two boys listened unobserved, Dwayne's astonishment grew when he realised they were speaking about me. From then on, he began to look upon my angel voices in a more thoughtful way, especially when I received forewarnings of events that were about to unfold in our lives.

Thankfully, most of these forewarnings related to simple domestic problems and usually meant something like a visit to the garage if it concerned our car. I had learned to ignore such warnings at my peril. One day, when I received a message from Angel Ann that the brakes on Fran's taxi were faulty, I rang him immediately.

'Don't pick up another fare,' I said. 'Go straight to a garage. Your brakes are faulty.'

He told me the car had been checked recently and the brakes were fine. As soon as he finished our call, a man approached him and signalled that he wanted a lift. Fran was about to open the door when he decided to take my advice. He refused the fare and drove away. He had only gone a short distance down the road when his brakes snapped. Fortunately, he was able to control the car and bring it to a halt. It was the last time he ignored a warning from the angels.

But his credulity was strained to the limit on the morning I saw a picture of a large swan in my mind's eye. I couldn't banish the image and when Fran was leaving for work I said, 'You're going to pick up a strange fare today.'

'Who's that going to be?' he asked.

'A swan,' I replied and was not surprised when his is-my-wife-crazy-or-what? expression came over his face.

However, during that day as he was driving along North Frederick Street, he was forced to stop when a large and defiant swan stood in the centre of the road. The swan had probably strayed from the Royal Canal or the nearby Blessington Street Basin Park, and the crowd who had gathered around it were trying to decide what to do.

Fran is a big guy, strong and decisive, with twenty years' soldiering behind him. Without too much fuss, he managed to capture the swan and bundle it into the boot of his taxi. Being a bit of a comedian, he stopped off at the Irish Taxi Drivers' Federation, which was nearby, and called in to report that a passenger he had picked up on North Frederick Street was refusing to pay his fare. When some of the staff came out to investigate Fran suggested they check the boot. Fortunately, no one collapsed from a heart attack when the boot was opened and the swan lunged upwards. They appreciated the joke and rang the ISPCA to ask for an official to come and return the swan to its rightful home.

Angel Ann continued to influence our lives. She told me that Jason, our eldest son, has a strong psychic awareness. Some day, he may decide to tap into this force, but that will not happen until he has lived the life of a young man and done all the things he needs to do. Whether or not he decides to open himself to that work is up to him. No pressure is ever applied by the angels. We can accept or reject the guidance they offer us.

But one such psychic occurrence took place about eight years ago when he was a young teenager. He was asleep one night when he awoke and saw an apparition standing in the corner of his bedroom. He cried out with shock and when we rushed to see what was wrong, he was sitting bolt upright in his bed, his eyes fixed on a certain spot.

'Can you see the boxer?' he asked.

Fran and I were unable to see anyone or anything. He described a young man dressed in boxer shorts and wearing boxing gloves. His stance was that of someone preparing to fight but there was nothing menacing about him. This manifestation appeared for the next five nights. Once Jason recovered from his initial shock, he accepted the apparition and was no longer frightened.

On the sixth day, I did a reading for a woman who had booked the appointment a week previously. She turned out to be the mother of a well-known Irish boxer. The following morning, I asked Jason if the boxer had appeared again. He said he hadn't and Jason has never seen him since. I can only assume that this psychic connection was created when the boxer's mother booked her appointment.

I'm very fortunate that my extended family are watched over by a wonderful, gentle soul called Margaret. She has been a loving and spiritual presence in my life for about ten years. She was a mother on this earth and her nurturing love for her family still reaches out beyond her spiritual boundaries. I never knew Margaret (who is affectionately remembered in her family as Peggy). She was Fran's aunt and she appeared to me in my bedroom one morning, accompanied by her granddaughter Sinead and her husband Timmy, who was called 'Uncle Duckegg' by his nieces and nephews. Margaret asked me to tell Maggie, her daughter, that they were together and happy in the spirit world. She held a gold bracelet in her hand. I knew this was significant and that the information should be passed on to Maggie. I was right. Maggie explained that on the death of her daughter Sinead, Maggie's father Timmy had bought two gold bracelets. Margaret was still alive at the time and he gave one to her. Maggie received the other one.

Maggie was touched and comforted by this message, especially by the knowledge that Sinead was with her grandparents. Time passed before Margaret came to see me again. Maggie was very ill. Her time on earth was coming to an end and Margaret wanted her family to know that she was with her daughter at this critical time.

I attended Maggie's funeral and it took my breath away when I saw a vision of her with her parents and her lovely daughter. They looked so happy and peaceful together, all of them reunited at last.

In October 2008, when I was living in Spain, I encountered Margaret again. When she comes, I feel her breath in my right ear and the most piercing pain shoots through it. The pain disappears as soon as I acknowledge her presence. On this occasion, her daughter-in-law Rita was seriously ill. Margaret told me that Rita would soon be leaving us and returning to her heavenly home. She began to relay names of certain people associated with Rita, who had passed over into the world of light. I wrote them down in case I forgot them. She told me to tell Noel, her son and Rita's husband, that he should light candles to comfort Rita. Margaret wanted him to know that she was looking after them and would bring them comfort at this time of sorrow. She also told me that a close friend of Rita's had placed a beautiful medal around her neck earlier that day.

I passed on this information about the candles and the medal to Noel, who confirmed that Rita had indeed received the medal that day. He also told me that Rita loved to see candles burning but for some reason no candles had been lit on that particular week. Margaret must have known how important it was for Rita to see the light radiating from those candles.

Perhaps as we approach our final moments, burning candles represent our own inner light, which will always keep alight. Not all of us will have the comfort of dying among our loved ones, or have candles lit for us. Our death may be sudden and tragic, and we will have no time to say goodbye. If this is to be our fate, then I believe we have a different light. The light of an angel standing there with us at that final moment, showing us that we do not die alone. We are always in God's care when he calls us home.

Two weeks later, after Margaret's visit, I was to encounter her again. She came to tell me that Rita had passed away. She was now with her extended family, whose names had been relayed to me during Margaret's earlier visit. Yes, there was sadness within the family Rita had left behind. They were a family where much love had flowed between them and I knew that Rita would be watching over them. I said goodbye to Margaret and thanked her for letting me know.

I love Margaret's soul, her enthusiasm when she visits me. I don't like the pain in the ear, but it is worth that slight discomfort to communicate with her. A few weeks after Rita's death, I returned to Ireland and visited her family. When I arrived at their home, Margaret and Rita were waiting for me. They communicated many messages to me, information I could not possibly have known in advance, and the healing this gave to her family was a blessing from the angels.

When Margaret contacted me again, I was in Ireland touring with my book *My Whispering Angels*. I had just finished doing some angel readings in Limerick and Fran was driving back to Wexford where we planned to stay for a short while. Rain was falling and dark clouds veiled the sky. We were passing through Carrick-on-Suir when I, once again, experienced that piercing pain in my right ear. Before I had time to welcome Margaret, she introduced herself. Her energy was heavy as she came around me and I instinctively knew that something was wrong.

All she said was, 'Eddie is not well.' Then she was gone. I did not understand this message and I had no idea who Eddie was. Fran looked thoughtful when I repeated her brief words to him. He told me that he knew two Eddies. One was Margaret's brother, who was his uncle, and the other was his cousin, Margaret's son. I intuitively understood that the message concerned Margaret's brother. We stopped the car and phoned Fran's mother, Patricia, who was also Eddie's sister. Her phone was engaged and we had to wait for a few moments before ringing again. This time we got an answer and discovered that at the precise time Margaret had spoken to me, Eddie was on the phone to Patricia. Fran relayed the message I had received from Margaret but, according to Patricia, Eddie's health seemed fine. But she was wrong. Eddie was quite ill but had not told any of his family. Sadly, ten days later he passed away.

Could Margaret have told me more? Maybe given me some information that might have extended Eddie's life for a while longer? I do not believe so. Eddie's time had come. It is God's will to choose when we leave this physical world.

Margaret came back to thank me for being there whenever she needed to reach out to her family. She is a beautiful soul who can remind us all that life is far from over when we pass away. I know as I continue my journey here in the physical plain, she will continue to communicate with me. I thank her for making me the spiritual conduit between her and her loving family.

4

Dealing with Negativity

*Every time we have a negative thought, we should
observe it, accept it, release it. If we accept our negative
thoughts but do not engage with them, we take control
over them and replace them with positivity.
But if we feed our negativity, engage in a conversation with it,
then we are handing power over to our egos.*

IT IS IMPORTANT THAT I PREPARE MYSELF FOR AN
angel reading. My mind needs to be clear, my senses attuned
to the information I will receive from Angel Ann. In the
mornings, I pray and meditate. I end this session with a strong
visualisation. My favourite visualisation is to imagine myself
within the solitude of a forest where I am surrounded by the
harmony of nature. Everyone has a favourite place where they
can travel in their imagination and be at peace.

We have seven main energy centres, which are called
chakras. They start at the base of the spine and travel upwards

through the head. We have numerous minor chakras, often referred to as meridians, which can be stimulated during acupuncture to attune our energies. Our primary chakras are listed as base, sacral, solar plexus, heart, throat, brow and crown chakras. They influence our emotional or spiritual health and can create an unbalance in our bodies that may, in time, manifest as a physical ailment. The seven colours of the rainbow are associated with each of the chakras and I refer to them as my 'seven bridges of light'. They are energised when I meditate, and empower me when I'm preparing to link with my angels. When I have finished my meditation, I am engulfed in a brilliant white force that has the strength of a shield. Within this space, I then visualise my forest. I enter it and sit peacefully within the trees where I wait to welcome my angels. (Visualisation and meditation are important exercises that are included in Chapter 12.) This visualisation brings me to a place of stillness, where my mind is ready to receive all that will be revealed to me. When it is complete and I am ready, I call my angels to me.

I sense them gathering around me. The sensation that there is someone standing behind me, and on either side of me, intensifies. When I experience this feeling, I ask the angels to blend their light and their energy with mine. Usually it is a subtle vibration but, sometimes, when I am making this connection, my energy changes and the vibrations build up so intensely in my legs that I can feel them shaking. This powerful momentum continues until it seems as if I have gone through an invisible barrier where my energy and the energies of my angels have blended together. We are one vision, one voice.

'Please let me be your voice,' I say. 'Please let me be your light. Please let me be your messenger.'

I am then prepared for whatever my day will bring.

Before beginning an angel reading, I explain to the person who has come to see me that three things can occur. Members of the person's family who have passed on may make contact, but I cannot always guarantee that this will happen. Secondly, the reading could be focused on the person in front of me, concentrating on the blocks in their lives that they need to challenge. Thirdly, there may be no reading. Thankfully, this is a very rare occurrence but, if it happens, people immediately worry and assume I have seen a tragedy coming their way. This is absolutely not the case. It could simply be that the timing is not right for them. Or their lives are going the right way and nothing needs to change.

When I finish a reading, I take a few minutes before the next person enters to clear out any negative energy that may have built up in the room. I light an incense stick and allow its fumes to purify the air. Then I am ready to begin anew. At the end of the day, when my work is over, I am tired but it is a charged tiredness that only affects my body. My mind is still as open and receptive as it was at the beginning of the day. I could continue reading and communicating with people but

Angel Ann advises against it. To close myself down is vitally important for my own well-being. Sometimes, I forget I am off duty, so to speak, and, from force of habit, I turn to her for advice or information. On such occasions, she refuses to assist me. This is for my own protection, to pace myself and give me the space to relax and prepare myself for the next day.

I'm often asked how I cope with angels in my life. What about my personal time, my intimate, private moments when I need to be alone – or with my husband in the privacy of our bedroom? When I want to have a private conversation with family or friends? When I want to have a shower? Do angels hover over the bathroom? Such an idea is unnerving to anyone – and I'm no exception to the rule. But Angel Ann assures me that this is not an issue.

Angels are available to us when we call them. They come when we want to communicate with them and leave when we wish to be alone. I often joke that they are nine-to-five workers. That is why I close myself down after a day of readings. Like my angels, I clock in and I clock out.

Sometimes, the lives of people who come to me for readings are so tragic and hurtful that I want to follow them and help in my own limited way. I will tell them to email or ring me, but Angel Ann believes that I should only go so far. If I am pulled in too many directions, I will, despite my best intentions, become ill and burned out. Ultimately, it is up to the person who seeks an angel reading to make their own decisions.

When a young man called James came to see me one evening, he was filled with negativity. A dark cloud surrounded him. I became aware of it as soon as he entered the room. I asked Angel Ann why this cloud was so dense and destructive. She told me that he was at a very distressed stage in his life and believed he would be better off if he passed on in the spirit world. As James sat down in front of me, Angel Ann made me aware of a soul standing behind him. This was James's father, who had come to communicate with him. But James did not want to listen to the messages from his father. He only wanted to die. At that moment, many angels began to surround him. They showered him with their love and healing. Angel Ann pointed out that James had so much more to accomplish along the way. His life was vitally important. He had many gifts, good health, a beautiful family and friends who loved him. He had a rewarding job and was highly admired by the people who employed him. He showed compassion and understanding to so many people and was always ready to lend a helping hand. James agreed that my angel was outlining the many blessings in his life, but all he saw was doom and gloom. He worried about the past, about the people he believed he had let down by not being good enough – or not being there when they needed him.

I knew that James was finding it almost impossible to focus on the positive aspects of his life. Angel Ann was doing her best but, at the end of the day, he had free will to make his own choice. Before he left, I suggested that he should see a counsellor, someone who might take him from the dark place that occupied his mind. He was adamant that nobody could help him. There were many angels with him when he left and I knew they would do their best to guide him.

Some days later, he came back to see me. He had gone home and thought about everything Angel Ann had said to him. As he did so, he felt this beautiful presence around him. It was peaceful and comforting, as if someone was encouraging him to live his life to the full. He wanted to open himself to the guidance of this angel who was encouraging him to seek counselling.

James returned to see me some months later. What a transformation. Through his counselling, he had become able to understand the destructive emotions he had carried for so long. It helped him appreciate the things that were important to him. He still reaches out to help people, but has learned that he can only do his best. Now he focuses on what he can achieve, rather than setting himself impossible goals and beating himself up when he doesn't achieve them.

Some weeks after James's visit, another person who was at a dangerous crossroads came to see me. Sonia suffered from the same self-disapproval and punishing negativity. Nothing made her happy. She was constantly focused on the many mistakes she had made at different stages in her life. She believed in the power of angels and was always looking for their guidance, but somehow she had never been able to find the answers she needed. Despite the fact that she was in a loving relationship, she believed she was drifting and that something essential was missing from her life.

Angel Ann showed me that she was an artist, a very good one, and this was only one of her many creative gifts. But she was not using any of them. She confessed that she never believed she was good enough to strike out on her own. Other people were always better. Angel Ann explained that this attitude was blocking her creativity. If she trusted in herself then the artistic gifts she possessed would sustain her financially.

The angel also reminded her that as a child she had loved to paint. She had enjoyed the freedom it gave her to express herself imaginatively but, over the years, people close to her had advised her that she would never make her living as an artist. She paid too much attention to those opinions and her life had taken her down pathways that could never fulfil her creative needs. Whenever she had had the urge to paint, she had listened to those voices who had so thoughtlessly told her she was wasting her time. They were wrong. Painting was her pathway to fulfilment. Her gift was still in her possession, all she had to do was believe how good she was and trust her own guidance. Sonia agreed with Angel Ann and decided to take stock of her life. She would return to that childish joy and enthusiasm, when she believed anything was possible. Today, she is a wonderful artist. She is also successful and people are buying her paintings. Most of all, she is enjoying every moment of her creative life.

Sometimes we have to let go and take that leap of faith. We have to trust that God and the angels will move the obstacles from our way so that we can achieve our full potential. When I made that leap of faith, I had to believe the words that Angel Ann channelled to me. Over the years, this trust continued to grow. So great is my belief in her guidance that even when the messages she communicates to me seem to make no sense to the person who has come for a reading, I will faithfully repeat them. Inevitably, they prove to be significant and true.

I was conducting angel readings one afternoon when two young women came together to the centre where I was working. I will call them Susan and Jean. Susan had requested a reading and she had her baby son with her. Jean intended to mind the little boy in the room next door while I carried out Susan's reading. This would be the last reading I would do that day. As I began to tell Susan what could happen during the session, I became aware that Angel Ann was shifting her energy towards the door. I was puzzled as I watched her light moving away from me. Also, I was receiving no information that I could channel towards Susan. This worried me. I was afraid this was going to be a non-reading.

Angel Ann finally spoke. She told us that Susan's life was blessed in many ways. It was Jean in the next room who needed her help. Would Susan consider allowing her friend to have the reading instead? Rather than being upset or disappointed, Susan immediately nodded and said she understood exactly what Angel Ann meant. She readily agreed to speak to Jean and persuade her to swap places. Jean was surprised but quite happy to sit for the reading.

Angel Ann had plenty to say that evening, and it all centred around an abusive and dominant relationship in Jean's life. Jean became very emotional as she listened to the information I was channelling. She admitted that she was in the depths of despair and did not know which way to turn for help. She had never spoken about this situation to anyone in her family and was relieved that the truth was finally out in the open. Angel Ann went on to reveal many more things to her and she agreed with everything that I communicated to her.

Even though angels will never interfere in a relationship, they try to guide us the best way they can. They know we have to follow our hearts and do what we feel is right for us. In this tragic case, Jean felt as if a great weight had been lifted from her. An angel had reached out and singled her for attention. The messages Angel Ann gave her were filled with hope and reassurances.

Angel Ann knew beforehand that Jean was coming, but I had no idea how things were going to develop when the two women entered my room. I would like to believe that her divine intervention encouraged Jean to begin her journey of healing. When she left that evening, Jean knew she was surrounded by the light of many angels and they would be with her every step of the way. But her future lay in her own hands. We are all gifted with free will to make our own decisions. Only we can determine by our actions if we can be happy and whole once again.

The world of the angels is not far away. It exists within the very core of our being and all we have to say is 'welcome'. The angels know about the pain and hurt we carry. They understand when we hesitate at crossroads, unsure of the direction we should take. They know how hard it is for us to let go of the things we no longer need and to make painful changes in our lives. Many people have spoken of the uplifting feeling they experience after listening to their angels. They have been given direction and guidance to seek out counsellors, healers and those who can help them let go of all the hurt they carry. Angels know that it is not always easy to heal. It takes time, but if we are willing to listen to those deep emotions that cause us pain, our lives can take a new direction.

Jennifer had not left her house for two years. Her agoraphobia was so great that it totally dominated her life. She was persuaded to come and see me and, although she found it very difficult to make the journey, with the help of her friend she arrived for her appointment. As soon as she began to talk, I knew that I would only be able to go a certain distance with her. Angel Ann quickly informed me that I did not have the experience to deal with the many issues in Jennifer's life. They had brought her to this stage of pain and isolation, and she needed professional help.

Jennifer agreed that she needed serious counselling, but she was unable to afford it. I took her number and contacted some people I knew who would be sympathetic to her problems. A counsellor agreed to see her for a nominal fee. The counsellor lived close to Jennifer, which was an added bonus.

Six months later when I was in a supermarket, I was approached by a woman whom I didn't recognise. It was Jennifer. She looked wonderful, assured and relaxed. She had received tremendous help from her counsellor and said that this help was ongoing and that she was still in a process of healing. About eight months later when I saw her again, she was radiant with good health and confidence.

'Only for you and the angels, and the help of my counsellor, I would still be in that dark place,' she said.

I appreciated her comments, but she was the person who had turned her life around. She had stayed with her counselling, forced herself to leave her house for each session and endured the pain of understanding the issues that had blocked her for so long. I've seen Jennifer a number of times since then, and she has truly blossomed from the distressed and confused person who first came to see me.

5

A Touch of Hands

This light that you cannot see resides within you. Reach into that energy, trusting that, at all times, it will hold you together. Seek it daily so it may light your way.

THROUGH MY WORK WITH ANGELS, I DISCOVERED that I did not have to sit with someone physically to be able to receive information relating to their lives. The first time I made this discovery, Fran had been approached by a work colleague, whom I'll call Declan, and asked if I would do an angel reading for him. Declan was self-conscious, embarrassed to admit that he wanted to receive messages from the angels. So great was his awkwardness that he did not want to meet me. Instead, he wanted me to give him a reading without him being present. I suggested to Fran that he bring me something that belonged to Declan and I would see if I could receive any information from it. I was highly amused the following day when Fran arrived home with Declan's cap. To avoid any of his own energy interfering with the cap, Fran had asked Declan to place it in a plastic bag.

My amusement quickly died away when I touched this cap and began to concentrate. Almost immediately, I was overwhelmed by strong impressions. I knew there was alcohol in Declan's life and it was a destructive force. It was also linked to aggression and this aggression had created great difficulties and sadness for his children. I saw a motorbike and a serious accident that Declan had suffered in the past. There were many scars on his body. I wrote down all my impressions and gave them to Fran to pass on to him. Declan was amazed by their accuracy. Everything I told him was correct, including the advice from Angel Ann that he needed serious counselling if he ever hoped to get his life back on track. Did he follow this advice? I've no idea. My work was done. It was up to him to decide what to do of his own free will. For me, this reading was a personal victory. It was the first time that I had been able to envisage someone's life without the person sitting opposite me. It would be the beginning of many such instances.

Sometime later, I received a phone call from a woman in America. She had spoken to a man who had visited me for a reading. He was hoping to establish a business venture in Ireland, but Angel Ann had advised him that his project would have more success in the United States. He had moved there and this woman (I will call her Beth) had invited him to dinner in her house. During their meal, he had discussed the reading with her. She asked me if I could do a similar reading over the phone. I had never attempted such a challenge, but I wrote down her name.

Then I did the same meditation and prayer that I normally did when I was meeting someone in the flesh. I focused on the piece of paper with her name on it and asked Angel Ann to guide me. She gave me the information I needed. It was quite substantial and, as I wrote down the message, I was worried that there was no one present in the room who could validate what she was telling me. A chandelier with three little fairy figurines hanging from it was shining above me. I asked Angel Ann to tap the figurines if the information was correct. I waited, hoping to hear a tinkling sound from above me. I waited in vain. Not a tremor or a tinkle. Nothing to break the silence, apart for the internal voice of Angel Ann instructing me to ring Beth in America and read out what I'd written down. I made the phone call and read out the information that had been channelled to me. Everything I said made perfect sense to Beth. When the call ended, I thanked Angel Ann for guiding me.

'Francesca, trust me. I will never tap fairies on a chandelier for you to believe in my guidance,' she retorted, and I have never tested her since.

Sometimes such work has far more tragic overtones. More recently, I was contacted by a heartbroken family in Norway whose son had disappeared on his way home one night from a party. Weeks had passed without the police finding any traces of him. In desperation, his family had contacted a number of psychics to see if they could shed any light on his disappearance.

They sent me his photograph. When I sat with this photograph, I heard Angel Ann's voice directing me to reach for a pen and paper. I drew a map of a town in Norway. At that time, I had visited Norway once but I had never been to this town and knew nothing about it. Yet I filled in details about the streets that I later discovered were accurate. On the map, I drew a picture of a school. My thoughts kept tugging me towards it and I believed the young man had a strong connection to it. But I did not believe it was connected to his death.

While I was working on the map, I believed that his spirit was with me. I felt an entity around me and it was the strength of his presence that informed me that he was dead. It had been snowing the night he disappeared and I had a strong sense that he had slipped and lost his balance on his way home from the party. I could picture a harbour with a rock face wall and my impression was that he had fallen into the water. I also believed it would be three more months before his body was discovered.

I hoped I was wrong. I kept thinking about my own boys, and the worry I always felt when they lived at home and went out for a night with their friends. I found it very difficult to contact this family in Norway as I had no positive news. I imagined their desperation, their hope, no matter how fragile, that their son was still alive. I thought how policemen must have a similar feeling of dread when they have to knock on someone's door and break the news that a fatal accident has taken place.

His family were already resigned to the fact that he must have died that night. Their main concern was to locate his body. I emailed all the information that had been revealed to me, along with the map I had drawn. I discovered that the school I had seen in my mind's eye had been demolished some years previously and a block of apartments had been built on the site, and that this is where their son had lived. I also found out that there was a fishing harbour in the town and a lake.

A few months later, as I had predicted, his body was found. He had drowned in the lake, a simple but tragic accident. His family contacted me and told me that I was the only one who was able to give them a specific location. Their gratitude was genuine and touching. Their son had given me the name of a young woman and a message that I was to relate only to her. His family contacted her and she rang me shortly afterwards. Initially, I thought she might be his girlfriend, but it turned out that she had been his closest friend. She had also been the last person to see him alive.

He had communicated to me that he and this young woman had had a personal conversation that night and that he had confided certain personal information to her. She agreed that this had happened, but said she could not divulge what they had discussed. I assured her that I had no intention of invading their privacy but once I received a vital piece of information I needed to have it validated. A simple 'yes' or 'no' was all I required. When she agreed that the conversation had taken place, I told her that his spirit had asked me to thank her for listening to him so attentively.

Another request to find someone who was lost had a happier ending when I was contacted by the relation of the young woman, whom I will call Elise. Elise had disappeared during a continental holiday and her relations were extremely worried about her. I did not ask Elise's relation for any item of her clothing or jewellery. Instead, we just sat together and I asked Angel Ann to help.

As I spoke to my angel, an image flashed before my mind. I saw Elise in a boat. She was calling to someone and she appeared to be lost. I also knew that the reason for her disappearance was connected to some form of domestic abuse and it was influenced by drink. Both partners had an equal responsibility for the state of their relationship and the alcoholic problems they had developed. I could tell that they loved each other and were usually good together. But when drink was consumed, it was a different story.

Elise's relation agreed that this was true and I continued to describe what Angel Ann was telling me. Elise had had a row with her partner in their apartment. There had been some minor violence. Blood had been found on the floor. The police were questioning her partner, but I knew that he had not killed her. No serious injury had occurred and Elise was still alive. It seemed to me that she was confused, probably concussed, and she had no idea where she was. The drifting boat seemed symbolic of her confusion, and that image was replaced by a vision of her sitting on a park bench. All I could tell her relation was that, within three days, Elise would walk into a police station. And that was exactly what happened. She was suffering from concussion when she entered a police station in a different town from the place where she was last seen. In this instance the story had an ending that, if not exactly happy, offered this couple another opportunity to work out their personal problems. I hope they reached for that second chance and embraced it.

6

Doubts and Decisions

Was I truly a spirit of God or just someone searching for
the answers to her life? What was so deep within me
that I needed to find those answers? Why did He not come
when I cried out to Him? What had I done that He did not
come when the pain in my heart was so deep it crushed
everything inside me. Why did He not come?

SINCE I FIRST LISTENED TO THE VOICES OF
angels, I have been on an emotional and wondrous journey
with them. I have reclaimed the parts of myself that I lost when
I was looking after my home and family. I had been content
and happy during those early years but, along with the rewards
of being a mother and home-maker, there had been losses,
mainly an eroding of my self-confidence. The confidence I
had carried as a young woman had become eroded when my
children were small and I was fully engaged in looking after
them. I had lost a little more of myself each year, but now I was

rediscovering my old identity. I was taking back the freedom I had surrendered – and, as I took it back, I liked it.

What changes had Angel Ann and the angels wrought in me? I had listened to their voices, heeded their instructions and I understood that this personal journey was the most important one I would ever make. Angel Ann had asked for my trust and when I gave it to her, I was amply rewarded. With her help and encouragement, I was learning to let go of all I no longer needed in my life. I cannot pretend this was easy. Having stepped into their vibrational light, I loved the intense sense of wholeness it gave me. But Angel Ann did not grant me instant happiness or remove the pressure that comes with making life-changing decisions. I argued with her and, sometimes, raged against the direction in which she was guiding me. But I knew that there was so much more she could teach me.

I was drawn to the idea of holding angel evenings. I had come a long way since my initial attempt to interact with a live audience and I was convinced this was the next step I should take. To my surprise, when I asked Angel Ann to help me communicate with my angels in a public forum, she told me I would never develop my platform skills in Ireland. There were too many blocks and interruptions in my life. But if I moved permanently to Spain I would receive the spiritual guidance I needed.

Trust is vital when we are in communication with angels. Otherwise, nothing makes sense. Some years previously, Angel Ann had asked me to let go of my old way of life by the symbolic surrendering of my name. Our name is our badge of identity, our closest possession. It is not surprising that one of the most humiliating forms of torture and abuse is to replace a person's name with a number. Yet, when I was asked to surrender my name I did it willingly.

I had been guided to a mountain in Donegal where Angel Ann appeared to me and spoke about the journey I would undertake.

'When you got sick your soul cried out to go home to God,' she said. 'God took you home and revived your soul. I need you to let go of your name. As you journey with me you will be known as Francesca Brown.'

When she spoke that name it was like slipping on a glove and finding that it was a perfect fit.

Now I was being asked to surrender my home. Some years previously, Fran and I had bought a holiday home in Orihuela Costa in Spain. It was a delightful place to visit and we had enjoyed many holidays there. As a result of these visits, I had become acquainted with a number of spiritualist churches that had been established in Spain, mainly by British expatriates. Although I did not embrace the religion of the spiritual churches, I felt a kinship with their insightful and visionary beliefs in the spirit world. Courses in spiritual development, meditation and visualisation are held in these churches, as are demonstrations by well-known psychics and spiritual healers.

I had attended a course in meditation at one of these centres and had made contact with a warm and welcoming spiritualist minister. On the first afternoon I attended her course, she gave us a philosophical lecture on 'The Tree of Life'. When it was over, she handed me a piece of paper and told me to write about my own Tree of Life. I was confused as to what to write but she said, 'You are surrounded by angels. Ask them to explain your Tree of Life to you. Writing will become an important element on your spiritual journey.' The Tree of Life is your inner knowledge. From its trunk come many branches, and each represents a different part of your learning journey through life, on which you travel with your angels, helping you to define and acknowledge who you are.

I did as I was asked and read my essay out to the group. When I finished, the spiritualist minister asked me to give a message from the spirit world to someone in the room. This time, I felt confident in my ability to communicate with a wider group, and I did as she asked. When I finished, she told me that the journey I was taking with my angels would be incredible. She understood how I was struggling to understand the changes taking place in my life but believed that I would prevail with their support. Just before I left, she admitted that if she had been conducting a church service that evening, she would have asked me to participate in it and communicate with my angels. As I walked away from her workshop, I sensed a change in myself. I knew I was reaching another level of awareness but little did I realise the changes I would be expected to make.

Fran, understandably, was startled when I told him what I wanted to do. We were walking along the beach near our holiday home when I brought up the subject of moving. I heard the doubt in his voice as we discussed the possibility, but I also heard another voice, an internal voice that spoke with conviction and authority.

'Tell Fran he will become your eyes and ears while you work for us. Tell him he will receive a sign.'

That sign came on the last night of our holiday. The bedroom was dark when Fran woke. As he lay in the darkness, unable to sleep, he noticed a sphere of light at the end of the room. Two more smaller spheres appeared. As they grew more luminous, he heard a voice utter these words, 'Trust in us.' In the same instant, the lights faded. Instead of being scared, Fran was overjoyed, as he had been looking for this promised sign. I had slept through this experience, but he woke me and told me he was fully behind my decision.

On the flight back to Dublin, we were already planning our move to Spain. This meant pulling up roots, saying goodbye to our extended families and our many close friends. But hardest of all was leaving our sons behind. Jason and Dwayne were now young men. They liked Spain for holidays, but they had no interest in settling there permanently. They wanted to be with their mates and girlfriends in Dublin, and we totally understood this.

We sold our house without any difficulty and rented an apartment in the same location for the boys. At the end of June 2005, Fran and I moved to Spain. The enormity of my decision came to a head when the plane taking us from Ireland lifted off and I felt as if it was flying backwards, taking me back to the life I was leaving behind.

'What am I doing?' I asked Angel Ann. 'I've just thrown away everything I love to take this journey with you. I hope to God I've got this right.'

She assured me that my decision was the true one and, for a while, I was content. It was the same as being on holiday, except this time we had no return ticket.

Life in Spain was wonderful. Exactly as I had imagined. I loved the bright colours, the sun shining on the reddish-brown rooftops, the leisurely strolls in the evenings, the glistening sea. I had the peace and tranquillity I needed. Meditation came easy. I had time to write without the everyday distractions that had marked my life in Dublin. Another angel entered my life and appeared regularly to communicate poems to me. This was Angel Jonathan who had a scholarly approach, rather like a kind but firm teacher. Many poems were channelled through him and, to all intents and purposes, my life was running on track. It took me some time to realise that I was restless and becoming increasingly unhappy.

Our Spanish holidays always came to an end. Even as I said goodbye to the sun, I was already looking forward to returning home and getting back to my usual busy routine. But now this was my home. I couldn't meet up with friends for coffee, nip down to the shop for a few groceries, cook a meal for my boys and listen to their latest escapades. I was astonished by the depth of my loneliness, and also by my guilt. Even though our sons were at an age when they were striking out on their own, and had been quite excited by the idea of their new-found independence, it had been my decision, not theirs, to break up our family unit. Fran did his best to reassure me and keep me in touch with the reasons why we had made this decision. But the guilt, niggling and persistent, refused to go away.

Throughout this uncertain time, Angel Ann continued to encourage me, to convince me that all would be well in time. My uncertainty was fuelled by the fact that we had sold our family home in Dublin just before property prices began to spiral out of control. I could never imagine being in a position to buy a house again if we decided to return. Moving to Spain was proving to be an emotional and spiritual journey that, at times, laid me low or raised me up to great heights. I wrote and meditated, argued with Angel Ann and was occasionally swept low with self-pity. I'd lie on my bed and feel her stroking my hair, holding my hands. I can only describe this as a tingling sensation in my fingers, and when it occurred I was instantly filled with a deep sense of peace.

'Trust in the process,' she would say, which did not sound like a very angelic message but it was one I understood. For a while I would be carried along by her conviction, but then the doubts and the nagging loneliness would strike again. The guilt I had experienced over leaving our sons refused to go away. Angel Ann kept saying, 'Your biggest block is those boys. But they are well, they are coping and becoming independent.'

Every day I wrote for four or five hours. The voices of angels channelled their words to me. Sometimes their voices spoke so fast that I could not keep up with them and I would ask them to slow down. At other times, the sheer physical act of writing was so intense that I had no idea what message the angels wanted me to convey. But when the session ended, and I had time to look over that I had written, it all made perfect sense.

One night, when I was feeling particularly lost, I took Fran's advice and decided to visit a spiritualist centre I had attended on a few occasions when I had been on holiday. I wanted to do a meditation session in the comfort and company of like-minded people. I had always found this particular centre to be a peaceful place to visit and believed it would lift my mood. I was warmly welcomed by the woman leading the meditation. She recognised me from my previous visits and asked if I was on holiday. I told her I had moved here permanently and that I hoped to develop my spiritual connection with my angels.

A short while later, another woman attending the session spoke to me about her own psychic development. She described how she was building a successful reputation abroad and asked what I hoped to achieve by moving to Spain. I told her that

I had been guided by Angel Ann to make this move. To my astonishment and dismay, she said, 'You might as well pack your bags and return home. Nothing's going to happen for you here.'

As this person was supposed to have the insight of a psychic, her remark cut me to the quick. The woman running the centre overheard her remark but did nothing to intervene or contradict it. This increased my apprehension. Had I made a dreadful mistake? Did I really believe that, in a foreign country, I would find the enlightenment I sought? As these thoughts tumbled through my mind, I felt Angel Ann's wings wrap protectively around me. Her touch was as gentle as the brush of a feather and her voice was strong, commanding me to ignore what I had just heard. I left the centre shortly afterwards and cried bitterly on the drive home. I realised that the psychic/spiritual community has its flaws and petty jealousies, the same as any other community, but this woman's comments had added to my insecurity. I was developing a fear that what I had experienced in my communication with the angels would disappear and my life would return to normal. I had no problem with this normality, but having opened myself to this spiritual gift, I dreaded losing it.

This was my frame of mind on a sunny afternoon as I sat by the swimming pool and wondered if I had made the greatest mistake of my life.

7

A Divine Visitation

I am the light force that guides you on your journey of awakening.
In these days of loneliness and sadness, I have given you the motivation and courage to see this journey through.
Your purpose on earth is to seek the light that will help you accomplish all that lies within you. I am the spirit that contains your life, your journey, your purpose. I will help you to fulfil every dream that lives inside your heart.
The Voice of *Who Am I?*

IT HAD BEEN A STRANGE SORT OF DAY. SOMETHING was in the air, a lightness, an energy that seemed beyond my reach yet was waiting to reveal itself to me. Only one other person was by the pool, a woman sunning herself and oblivious to my presence. I was glad we did not have to make polite conversation. My mood was too low to indulge in idle chitchat.

I became aware that the energy around me was strengthening. I was attuned to the momentum and power of my angels but this was different to anything I had previously experienced. Was I apprehensive as I felt this force surrounding me? Yes. I did feel the tightening of tension within me, but I also experienced a deep sense of anticipation. I knew that something wonderful was about to transpire and it would affect me profoundly.

I saw him then, a powerful light force coming towards me. I understood instinctively that this was a male presence and the vibrations of energy emanating from him almost overwhelmed me. The sensation was so beautiful, so positive, that I felt uplifted. I was prepared to embark on a profound spiritual experience with someone very special.

I asked him who he was. I did not speak the words aloud. That is not necessary when I am communicating with angels.

'Who Am I?' he replied.

I repeated my question three times and he each time he repeated the words, 'Who Am I?'

I realised then that I was speaking to the divine presence within me. He was echoing my own doubts, the questions I kept asking myself as I struggled to adapt to a new way of living. Who am I? Where am I going? Am I losing touch with my angels? Everything seemed stalled in my life and he had come to bring me to a new awareness.

His voice sank deep into my consciousness. 'I am the light force that guides you in your journey of awakening. I have come to show you a world of truth. You have access to this world at all times. It contains the knowledge that you will hold when you are ready to open up to that channel. This journey is an awakening to the other lives that have guided you to where you are today. As you journey onwards, you will experience many spiritual encounters. They will awaken great shifts in your consciousness. As you experience each shift, you will reach a deeper understanding of your life's purpose. I am the knowledge and the wisdom that lives within you. On this journey, you will bring with you all of the gifts that you have accomplished along your way. You have the motivation and courage to see this journey to its end. The final outcome will be wonderful. I am the one truth that will guide you home.'

I have no idea how long he stayed with me. Time seemed meaningless as I listened to his words and absorbed his tremendous vitality. Dim and distant memories stirred within me. They did not belong to this life and I knew that this powerful presence was someone who had journeyed with me a long time ago. I had no clear recollections to confirm this belief. All I possessed was the conviction that I was welcoming home a long-lost friend. He had made his presence known to me so I could experience his love, his pure and illuminating wisdom.

His light faded and his voice was silent. I understood that a new spiritual presence had entered my life. Not an angelic presence but someone who had once walked this earth in another time.

'Who Am I?' he had said. I would call him by that name. It had a powerful resonance that echoed through my soul. I felt his love glowing within me. He would return to bring me into a deeper understanding of the path I was travelling with my angels.

The woman who had been sunbathing looked across at me. 'What was all that about?' she asked, and went on to describe the deep calm that had settled over her. She had been unable to move in that stillness and had had no idea what she was experiencing. Then, as if a switch had been turned off, the feeling disappeared and she had been snapped back to reality.

I no longer felt self-conscious discussing my communication with angels. But how could I explain to a stranger what had just occurred? As I wondered how I could reply she said, 'Do you mind if I ask you what you do?'

'I work with angels,' I replied.

'That explains everything.' She nodded, unsurprised. She did not ask any more questions or attempt to sensationalise her experience. Nor did she look for an angel reading, then or later, nor make any other attempt to impose on me. I still meet her occasionally and she always enquires if my angels are still in communication with me and refers to the amazing stillness and peace that settled over her that afternoon.

I was right to believe Who Am I? would return. I have come to know this beautiful light. I feel as if I have always been a part of him but I cannot remember how or where we met. Memories surface from time to time and I visualise places and people to whom I was once connected. Are they my family? Were we all together in another time, another space? I do not know if I left them, if I said goodbye. These memories are fragments, pieces of a jigsaw, long forgotten. I wonder when our paths first crossed. Did we form a friendship that has taken us from one journey into the next, inspiring each other to reach our goals and fulfil all that was within us? Did he accomplish his journey first and return to his eternal home before I was ready to go? Is he reaching beyond anything I can ever understand to hold my hand, to be my friend and guide? I believe that this wondrous spirit was sent by Angel Ann to strengthen my belief that I had made the right decision to settle in Spain. His loving words comforted me at a time when doubts threatened to overwhelm me.

He has been a wonderful mentor who has taught me to appreciate the importance of me, the importance of my own identity. The significance of that spiritual and physical identity we all possess but diminish by considering ourselves unworthy of the love God bestows on us. He makes me positive in my thoughts and actions, of my visions for my future. I believe that, one day, I will stand in a place of light and he will welcome me home. Perhaps, before then, as my awareness deepens, I will understand the links in the chain that bind us together.

'I am the knowledge and the wisdom that lives within you,' he said. 'I am all of you. I am your mind, your body, your spirit. I have never been separated from you.'

8

Spreading My Wings

The Tree of Life is you. It is many branches that you grow
as you begin your journey with spirit. Each branch carries
different books of learning and, as you grow, you take
the knowledge from each branch. It does not matter how
long the journey takes or the length of time you need to learn
these lessons. The Tree of Life is the essence of who you
are with spirit. As you grow stronger, the branches will begin to
merge together until you are all-knowing. You are one.
Extract from my 'Tree of Life' Essay

ANGEL ANN WAS RIGHT ABOUT MY SONS. THEY
may have received a tough reality check the first time the
electricity bill arrived or when they reached the supermarket
checkout, but they coped and became independent and self-
sufficient. In time, they moved on with their partners. When I
heard the news that they were leaving the apartment, I wanted
to be in Dublin to oversee the move into their new homes.

This was a symbolic desire, a need to witness the cutting of that protective, maternal cord. A furniture van arrived to take away their possessions, and then they were gone with their partners to take the next step on their own life journeys. I was more settled afterwards, contented that our lives had moved full circle and that it was just Fran and I again, as it had been in the beginning.

It took time to realise that I had emboldened myself by moving to Spain. I was conscious of standing in my own power. I wanted Fran to walk this journey with me but, if he decided to do otherwise, I knew that I was perfectly capable of walking it on my own. But Fran had opened himself to the concept of angels and their influence in our lives. He began to enrol in a number of courses to help him increase his understanding of his own psychic awareness.

I was guided to the sanctuary of the spiritual churches and the services they ran on Sunday mornings. Usually at such services, prayers are recited. There will be a philosophical lecture and some wonderful music. A spiritual demonstration by one of the congregation is held and that person will make contact with the world of light. I was asked by one of the ministers if I would consider conducting one of the Sunday services.

'Now it's time to spread your wings, Francesca,' she said.

I agreed to her request without hesitation. Afterwards, on reflection, I wondered if I had been right to agree so readily. Once my doubts set in, Angel Ann was there, as always, to strengthen my backbone. I asked her what I should speak about.

'You must speak about letting go,' she said.

'How can I speak about letting go?' I asked. 'I'd break down in tears because I'm only too well aware of what I've left behind me.'

But she persisted in encouraging me to take this subject as my theme. 'You let go, not just of everything that made you secure, but also your children,' she said. 'By letting go of the things you valued, you have become more conscious, more aware of this life force around you. In letting go, you become a part of this great universe where no judgement, no hatred, no injustice can touch you. For they exist only in your fears.'

I understood what she was telling me. We hold on to many worldly possessions that do us no good. They deflate our spirit. No matter what we possess, there will always be something missing. But if we choose to become more in tune with our spiritual beings, we will have everything we need.

I conducted the service and it was a wonderful experience. At the conclusion, I had to stand before the congregation and communicate with those who had passed on. It was the first of many services I would undertake and I loved this involvement within a community of people who were on the same wavelength as myself. They began to come to me for readings and angel demonstrations, which I conducted in the spiritual centres throughout the area.

Three years had passed since the incident that had deflated me in the spiritual centre. I was shopping in a Spanish market one day when I met the woman who ran it. We recognised each other and stopped to talk. I had not visited her centre since that night. By now, my reputation as an angel communicator was firmly established. She apologised for the incident and for not interjecting when the remarks were made. When I had not appeared again at her centre, she had assumed I had returned to Ireland. I outlined the work I had been doing, particularly my involvement in the spiritual churches. She had not known my name and when she heard who I was, she was astonished. She knew about Francesca Brown but had not realised I was the same dejected person who had left her centre that night.

She rang me later to ask me to hold a demonstration for her group. I was confident and happy to agree. When it was over she said, 'I'm so glad you didn't go home.' She echoed my own thoughts and made me even more aware of the need to hold firm to our own self-belief.

I have been asked many times to explain how I communicate with angels. I can only describe their presence as a massive build-up of a positive and empowering energy. I am so attuned to their momentum that I can usually recognise which ones are with me by the currents of energy flowing around me and the luminous colours that float in the air. I know instantly if an angel is male or female. This is not something I have studied. Everything I know has been self-taught or passed on to me by

Angel Ann. She still appears to me in the form of a winged angel. Her appearance is symbolic of the angels I saw in pictures when I was a child and it was vitally important to see her in this form during the early days of her manifestation. Nowadays, I no longer need her to appear in this form. My belief in her presence is unconditional, like my love for her, and, more often, she now appears as a stream of brilliant light.

Many angels will be with me throughout my readings, but Angel Ann is the divine contact between me and the person who came to hear her. During the reading, she stands slightly behind me and speaks into my right ear. I speak to her, ask her guidance, before I begin the reading. This is an internal dialogue and I hear her words distinctly in my mind. I faithfully relate back to the listener what she is telling me. I believe she is my bridge between our two worlds. She has gifted me with the vision to penetrate this world of light and bring messages from loved ones who have passed over. These visions and messages take many forms and it is Angel Ann who decides which spirit will communicate with me. When a soul comes forward to speak, she takes a step backwards and I hear the voice of this departed spirit through her words. This is akin to a three-way conversation and I have learned to trust whatever she tells me, even if, in the beginning, her words did not make sense to the listener. Inevitably, when the message is analysed, it proves to be correct. I have learned that no matter how strange or unbelievable the message sounds, I should pass it on.

A funny example of this certainty happened when I had to do a reading for four sisters. When they were seated before me, I was aware that their mother had entered their space. According to Angel Ann, she was passing on a most unspiritual greeting from the spirit world to her daughters.

'I see you have the four bitches with you,' she said.

I stared in consternation at the four women seated in front of me. 'I can't repeat that,' I told Angel Ann. 'It's rude and insulting and not what they would want to hear from their mother.'

But I could feel this energy emanating from Angel Ann and her voice saying, 'You must repeat it.'

I sighed, but knew better than to ignore this voice, so I said to the women, 'I'm sorry about this but I have a lady here and she is identifying herself as your mother. However, she is referring to you all as "the four bitches".'

To my relief, they laughed uproariously and one of them said, 'That's our mam, without a doubt.'

It turned out that they had all been very close to their mother and any time she was expecting them to visit her she would say to her friends, 'The four bitches are coming to see me.'

It was a term of endearment and when they heard that particular phrase, it spoke volumes to them. They were happy when they left me and had no hesitation in believing that their mother had reached out from the spirit world to greet them.

On another occasion, I was visited by a woman, whom I will call Imelda, who told me a tragic story. Her dearly beloved brother had committed suicide. She was heartbroken and in need of reassurance that he was okay. She was afraid that his decision to die by his own hand had condemned him to hell.

I spoke to Angel Ann and asked for her assistance. Usually, at the beginning of a reading, I close my eyes and ask the person with me to do the same. A screen appeared in my mind's eye and I can only describe what happened as similar to watching a film. I recognised a hospital ward. It was filled with angels and they were tending to someone. I was unable to make out who it was. While I was trying to understand what I was being shown, the scene changed. I saw a hospital corridor with people sitting on seats along the walls. They appeared to be waiting for news of someone who was ill. I understood that I was in the spirit world and the images I saw were being interpreted to me through a human vision I could understand. The people began to introduce themselves to me. I called out their names to Imelda. She recognised the names of her parents and other deceased members of her family. I called out another name and it turned out to be her son, who had died when he had been a young child.

Again, the scene changed and I was back in the ward. But before I could see who was receiving such care from the angels, a curtain was pulled across. I asked Angel Ann why this had happened and was told that the time was not right for revelation. I admitted to Imelda that I had no clear idea what was going on and my 'earthly' interpretation was that this tragic victim of suicide was receiving care and counselling from the angels. While this was happening, his family in the world of light were gathering to greet him. Perhaps the angels were helping him in his transition by bringing him an understanding of why he had found his journey on earth so difficult.

Understanding Imelda's fears, I asked the angels if he was in hell. I was told he was safe in their care. Knowing that he was with angels brought Imelda great comfort. She came back to see me a year later. This time, I had no difficulty communicating with this young man. He had wonderful things to say to her. He now understood his reasons for wanting to leave this earth and was happy in the company of his parents and younger sister.

The world of light reaches beyond time and space. Our angels show us that even in difficult times, they can reach out and show us that the bonds of love never die between the physical and spiritual worlds.

9

Working with the Archangels

Angel Ann is the teacher among the stars of light.
She entwines her light within my physical body so I may see
through her, speak through her. She is positive and truthful,
always providing me with the information I need when I am
working with people. Always doing her best to help the many
who reach out to hear her words.

RECENTLY, I WAS VISITED BY A HEALER WHO asked me to do an angel reading for her. When I finished the reading, she told me that, although I was surrounded by many angels, Angel Ann was the 'boss'.

I had no problem agreeing with her comment. Angel Ann is my intermediary between our two worlds, but I also have what I call 'my team'. These are angels who work with me and, together, they provide a wondrous vibration that can still shake me to the core of my being.

The archangels are powerful beings. They come from the

Source of light, which is God, and their purpose is to serve mankind. They are known as Archangel Michael, Archangel Gabriel, Archangel Raphael and Archangel Uriel. Each one had a specific role to assist us in our daily lives. The more we become familiar with these archangels and what their purpose is, the more they can help us.

I often work with the four of them together. They teach me to let go, to be more grounded and to remove negative thoughts. To work alongside them is a truly amazing experience.

Many people involved in communicating with angels have tremendous faith in Michael. When he enters during a reading, I see him as a strong blue light circling the person who is sitting opposite me. He does not speak, and sometimes when he arrives I worry that I will hear bad news. But he gives us strength and courage when we face the difficult times in our lives. He reminds me of a warrior, a sentinel with a sword that protects us. But he also helps us to cut the ties that bind us and hold us back, the destructive forces like bad relationships, drugs or alcohol.

Usually when he appears, I know that the person with me has a strong belief in him. 'You always talk to Michael,' I say and, as I expect, I discover that they have a tremendous attachment to him.

When we are lost or frightened, or in a dangerous situation, Archangel Michael is there to guide us. If we are going on a journey by plane, train, car or boat, he offers us protection.

When I am going out with family or friends, I ask him to put his blue light around us.

Never be afraid to call on him for assistance. He is with us at all times.

Archangel Michael
I come before you today and ask you
to surround me in your blue flame of light.
Please give me courage as I face
these difficult times in my life.
Help me to find my truth in all I do today.
Surround me with your love and protection
So that I may learn to heal and let go of
those wounds that I carry in my heart
And I ask you to help me face each day in my life
with strength, courage and faith.
This I ask of you.

Archangel Raphael represents the healing light of God. He will aid me when I am doing a spiritual healing. I know he is with me when I see his powerful green light emanating around the person who has come to me for help.

Those who are drawn to the area of alternative healing and spiritual counselling can always depend on Raphael's assistance. He is a healing force for those of us who hold on to past pain and trauma, who need healing after leaving a difficult relationship, or need to calm our mind, body and spirit. When we begin any healing process with Raphael, we should always talk to him about that particular area of our lives that needs healing.

O Archangel Raphael
I come to you today
and ask for your assistance
in helping me to heal those areas of my life
that cause me discomfort and pain
(name them)
whether they be physical, emotional or guidance.
Please help me to restore and balance
everything within me
so that I may feel the power of your healing light
surrounding me each day.

Archangel Gabriel is a most beautiful angel and has a wonderful sense of humour. Each time I seek his assistance, I am aware of a powerful energy surrounding me. It is filled with humour, light and a love for everything and everybody. Gabriel helps us to open up those pathways so we may understand our life's purpose. If we are contemplating a move of house or starting a family, if we are under psychic attack or on a spiritual journey, or about to make any lifestyle change, he is there to help. He lifts our negative thoughts and brings laughter into our lives when it is most needed.

Archangel Gabriel
I come before you today to seek
the guidance of your light.
Give me the motivation and courage
so that I may move forward in my life.
Open up that pathway
so that I may understand
the purpose of my life more clearly.
Help me to experience the joys of life so that
my life flows each day in peace and harmony.
This I ask of you.

Archangel Uriel is the shining one, the light of God. He brings us peace, tranquillity and harmony. If we carry anger towards others and it is destroying us, if we drift aimlessly and never find what satisfies us, if we are unable to hold down a job or get bored and distracted very easily, we should seek the help of Uriel. He is with us when our life may come to a crossroads and we are indecisive; if we have difficulty in relationships or if wish to help others, then Uriel is a beautiful and gentle archangel who has much to offer us in our daily lives.

Archangel Uriel
You are the light of God which lives within me.
Today I ask you to help me find
that peace in my heart
that I long for every day.

Show me that place within me
that causes me so much discomfort
and turmoil in my life
so that I may finally release it and let it go.
Taking my life once again into an area
where the tranquillity of the universe can live in me.
And today I ask of you
to please come close to me,
fill my heart with joy and peace
and let the flame of God's light
heal everything within me.

10

The Inner Child

Why do we make our lives so difficult?
Why do we close so many doors?
Why is it so easy to let the world pass by as
we sit here with our thoughts, our loneliness and our pain?
Some days, it is so hard to continue but if we listen,
we will hear the voice of spirit telling us
to pluck the courage from within ourselves.
Be strong and hang on.
Trust and believe in everything our angels show us.

WHEN A PERSON COMES TO ME FOR A READING, they are often going through a difficult time in their lives. These problems are affecting their self-confidence and self-esteem. When it is necessary during a reading, Angel Ann will take me back to the reasons why that person is struggling so hard. She will bring me to the time when this hurt was first created and I understand that whatever the traumatic event or damaging pattern that developed in childhood was, it was never healed. Even at a subconscious level, such memories have a profound effect on that person's sense of worth.

In recent years, I see the presence of this inner child with increasing frequency. I'm not sure if this is because of the damaging revelations of child abuse and the willingness to bring that distressing subject into the public domain for discussion or, perhaps, my communication with Angel Ann has given me a deeper insight into the hidden depths of people's pain.

Alyson came to see me some months after she had given birth to her first child. She and her husband had been longing for a child and this should have been the happiest of times. Instead, she was distraught over her inability to bond with her baby. Her family believed she was suffering from post-natal depression, but Angel Ann was able to pinpoint exactly what was wrong.

Alyson's inner child stepped out from her as soon as I began the reading. This vibration of light was so intense that I understood instantly that as a child she had been severely damaged.

Angel Ann spoke to me and I carefully repeated her words. 'You had a traumatic childhood,' I said. I could immediately see that I had connected with something central to Alyson's distress.

'How do you know?' she asked.

'This little girl who has stepped out from you is very

frightened, very vulnerable and extremely unhappy. This is not a child from the spirit world. This is you, your inner child. She is taking me back into the past and showing me that you were abused by a relative. You have found it impossible to talk to anyone about this, even to your husband.'

I have implicit trust in Angel Ann and I repeated this very sensitive information. Alyson broke down and began to cry. She admitted that it was the first time she had ever discussed this trauma with anyone. The block that was preventing her from bonding with her baby was an innermost and terrifying dread that she might harm her child in that same abusive fashion. Although her fear was groundless, it was a negative force within her, made more potent by the fact that she had kept what had happened to her secret. Her husband was unable to understand her reaction to their new child, and Alyson was convinced that she was the most vile person imaginable.

Angel Ann reassured her that there was no fear she would harm her own child. Such fears were caused by this residual pain that had remained with her since childhood and was causing her to have such dreadful fantasies. As Angel Ann spoke, I saw many angels in the room, all of them offering a healing energy to this troubled young mother. The main message I wanted to get across to Alyson was that the past was not her fault.

After the reading, Alyson made a decision to talk to her husband and also to seek counselling. Some years later, I was delighted to hear that she had gone on to have another baby.

I know that she was able to bond with this child without the unhappy and distressing fantasies that haunted her when her first child was born.

When I do a reading, I can touch on the reason for a person's unhappiness but I cannot perform a miracle. All I can do is pinpoint the source of that pain and advise that person to seek healing through a trained counsellor or therapist. It was Alyson's choice to seek help and heal her inner child. Angel Ann guided her back to that horrific time, but Alyson brought herself to a place where she felt worthy to bond lovingly and confidently with her first-born.

Each day that I communicate with the angels, I understand that death is really just the beginning of our lives. One encounter that has always stayed with me concerned a young man, I will call him Keith, who came to see if an angel reading would help him find some direction and purpose to his life. As Keith sat down in front of me I saw that inner child in all his abject vulnerability. I also noticed the spirit of a man standing next to Angel Ann. She told me that this was Keith's father, who wanted to speak to his son. I was unsure if Keith wanted to hear from him. When his father was alive, there had been many negative issues between them. For most of Keith's young life, there had been a history of alcoholic and domestic violence in his family. He and his father never built a relationship and were like strangers to each other when his father died.

Angel Ann told me that Keith's father had done a lot of healing around himself in the world of light. Part of that healing was to be with his son that day. He was filled with regret over the way he had treated Keith, and he wanted to explain why he had been such a bad father. He too had seen only violence when he had been a young child. He had grown up in the belief that no one cared about him or loved him. The pathways he chose as he grew older were destructive, but he had no one to turn to for advice. No one to tell him he was making the wrong choices. He only knew that while he was in control, everything was all right. The hurt and pain that he had caused his loved ones while he was on this earth had left many scars behind. He was aware of this damage and he wanted to express his regret and sorrow.

I explained to Keith what was happening. It was important for him to listen to this spirit. But I could see his deep pain and resentment as soon as I mentioned his father's name. However, he agreed to listen. As his father spoke and Angel Ann relayed this information to me, I could see Keith's physical appearance change as he began to understand the conflicts that had raged in his father's heart when he had been alive.

Keith is also a father. His relationship with his son is completely different to the one he experienced as a child. It is good that the old destructive pattern did not continue with Keith, and this encounter with his father helped him to let go of his old pain and anger. Angel Ann gave him many directions, showed him pathways that would be beneficial to him. At the end of the reading he said, 'Please tell my father I forgive him.'

I asked Keith to say the words himself. His father was now standing next to his son and he would hear them. As Keith addressed those words to his father, I knew that a great healing was taking place between them. A loving relationship could begin, one in the spiritual world and one in the physical world. Keith had never expected his father to come through that day or to speak to him so openly. He thanked me and left. As he walked away, I knew that this reading would have a profound effect on his life over the coming months and I thanked Angel Ann for her intercession.

On another occasion, this inner child was visible to me as soon as a young man sat down in front of me. His father was still alive and I knew that his son continually sought his affirmation. I could hear sounds, loud voices, doors slamming, dishes breaking. I sensed much brutality and indifference in Steve's life – and he received no love from his father. Steve was now an adult but he still had the yearnings of a child. His unresolved relationship with his father was preventing him from forming positive bonds with others. Angel Ann told me that this relationship would never be sorted out. Steve's father was incapable of affection. Perhaps this was because of his own unresolved issues from childhood but, whatever the reasons, Steve had to stop seeking that affirmation. He had to move beyond the blocks that were damaging him. Angel Ann advised him to seek help. To look to the future, not the past. To move beyond that most fundamental need – to seek the love of those who are our flesh and blood – and look for that missing love within himself. To love himself and allow that love to reach out to others who were deserving of it and would use it wisely.

11

Journeying Towards the Light

To look upon a child is to look upon the innocence that still exists within us. Never discourage them if they say they have an angel by their side. To them, this is the most natural thing in the world. They are so open and aware of who they are, filled with the knowledge and understanding that we are more than what we see. They understand they are not alone and that to know an angel is a true gift from God.

EVEN THOUGH I DO NOT READ FOR CHILDREN, Angel Ann has sat with them and sometimes spoken to them. I always ask a parent's permission before Angel Ann reveals the names of their guardian angels. But, sadly, tragically, some children leave us early, and we are lost and heartbroken without them. The angels say that every child belongs to God, who embraces them when he welcomes them home. But these children are always aware of who they are, where they come from, and the loved ones they have left behind. All I have ever experienced in my communications with children who have passed on has convinced me that this is true. They live in the eternal light of happiness.

In *My Whispering Angels*, I wrote about a little spirit child Joanna who appeared to me in my home in Dublin. She explained who she was and why she had come to see me. I liked Joanna straight away. She was a mischievous little spirit and has helped me so much in my work with the angels. When I first encountered her, she was seven years old. She has grown up since then and often reminds me that she is now a young woman. But to me, Joanna will always be that little girl who came to me when I first started this journey. She is still mischievous and her light is so beautiful that I am glad that she walks with me, however old she is.

One particular day, when she came to visit me, she was accompanied by three other children. Joanna told me that they were her friends and that they lived and played together in heaven. She pointed to one of the children. He was a young boy and he seemed very happy. She asked me if I knew him.

'How can I know him?' I replied. 'He is from the world of light.'

'His name is Ben,' Joanna replied. 'He is your little boy.'

Her words took my breath away. I choked up with tears as I realised that this was the soul of the little boy I had miscarried and called Ben. Seeing my son, whom I never held in my arms, was an aching experience. His life had crossed over at such an early stage yet he lived on, both in my heart and in heaven.

When the children disappeared, I wondered if Joanna would ever bring him to me again. I thought about the children who pass over into the spirit world and the everlasting memories they leave behind.

This brought to mind an incident that happened when I was a young mother living in Finglas, where Fran and I lived when we were first married. Our house was close to where I had lived as a child, and the incident I am about to relate happened years before I first heard the voices of angels.

Fran and I were woken up in the early hours of the morning by the sound of a ball bouncing up and down. The sound seemed to come from our bedroom but, apart from us, the room was empty. It was only five o'clock and we had to assume that our boys had got up early to play. The bouncing, repetitive sound we heard must be coming from the back garden. A quick check revealed that Jason and Dwayne were both fast asleep in their beds. We had no idea where the noise was coming from. Fran went into the back garden to see if the children next door were playing with a football. Everything was quiet and there was no sign of children anywhere. Unable to understand what was going on, we went back to bed. The sound of the ball soon faded and we fell asleep again. When we woke, we would have believed we were dreaming, except that to have had two identical dreams was too much of a coincidence.

This occurrence was to continue for the next five mornings. Each time we got up to investigate, but could not work out what was going on. Yet the sounds remained clear and unmistakable. Fran noticed that the house where the neighbouring boys lived had been locked up and showed no signs of life. We later discovered that one of the boys had taken ill and had been hospitalised. His family had been with him all that week so that ruled out any possibility that the young lads had been playing games.

On the Friday morning, I returned home after bringing my sons to school. On entering the living room, I came face to face with a small blond-haired boy sitting on my wicker chair. He was smiling in my direction and casually swinging his legs. Then, as suddenly as I had seen him, he disappeared. I knew this was not my imagination. For whatever reason, I had witnessed a vision from beyond.

But who was he? Why had he come? Had he been bouncing that ball in our bedroom and reaching out from the world of light to communicate with us?

Suddenly I remembered that, when I was much younger, the son of a family on our road had died in hospital. He was very young, just a little boy, and news of his death cast a deep sadness over the local neighbourhood. For most of the young ones, it was their first experience of death and that was why the memory came back to me so forcefully.

I decided to approach one of our priests to discuss this vision with him. When I described what I had seen, he looked at me in a slightly alarmed way. I had expected that reaction and was not upset by it. What I had told him was mystifying and he was probably wondering if he was dealing with a crazy parishioner. A second man had been present in the church while I was speaking to the priest. He overheard our conversation and when I mentioned the name of the child who had died so many years previously, he brought me to a pew with a brass engraving. It was dedicated to this little boy. I discovered from the dates on the plaque that he would have been twenty-one years old that weekend. I was deeply touched by this discovery and wondered if he had returned to a house that held a special memory for him. Did he want us to acknowledge him so that we would also celebrate with him?

I offered the priest a small donation to say a mass for his soul. The priest agreed to perform the ceremony. We blessed his birthday when the day arrived. I never saw that little boy again.

But I was to see my son Ben again – and in the most amazing circumstances. I had been aware for some time of an Archangel called Melchizedek. His power was strong. I believed he was lighting the road before me so that I would understand everything he was about to reveal. Archangel Melchizedek brought me into a garden. In this vision, I was surrounded by an incredible beauty. The sights and scents enraptured me, and a memory buried deep within me vibrated through my soul. As I tried to capture those memories, a light touched me. I saw my father, a man whom I had loved dearly, but who had died years before from cancer. He reached out to embrace me, to welcome me briefly into his world.

I became aware of a little boy holding his hand. He smiled at me. I recognised Ben. The cry that came from me was wrenched from the centre of my heart. I looked at my son and my father and knew that everything was well. Ben was being cared for by my father, just as my father had cared for me in his earthly life. My tears became peaceful. I knew that, one day, I would be reunited with them. Ben reached out to hold my hand and I embraced him. I felt his love entwined with mine. He called me 'Mum'. The word sounded beautiful to my ears. I wanted to hold on to him and never let him go. He asked me to walk with him. We moved slowly through this beautiful garden. It was so comforting to hold his hand, to kiss his cheek that had only ever been touched by radiance. He has experienced much in his world of light but his experiences are filled with peace, contentment and happiness. He knows no pain, no separation, no loss. It is only our world that contains these things.

In this garden, I met many children. They spoke to me, each defining the purity of their lives. Ben's light was entwined with others, not only my father but the bonds of family. I saw a boy called Edward whose soul was carried into the light long before my own son journeyed home. Edward, who was born in 1960, was my husband's brother, a brother that Fran knew for only a short while. His family lived in a place called Corporation Tenement Building, known as The Buildings and nicknamed 'The Cage'. The area was also called Monto, this name made famous by The Dubliners through a popular street ballad 'Take Me up to Monto'.

Edward died when he was seven weeks old. When his mother lifted him from his carrycot to feed him, she noticed he was very pale and motionless. Edward's father immediately sent for his own mother, who lived nearby. But sadly nobody could do anything. Edward had passed during the night, his death caused by what is known today as Sudden Infant Death Syndrome. His parents were grief-stricken and Edward was buried in the angel plot in Glasnevin Cemetery. His small funeral was carried off with great dignity. His father and uncle carried his little white coffin on the back of a bike as they journeyed with Edward to his final resting place.

Edward's mother could not go with her son. In those days, there was an old wife's tale that the mother could not walk behind the coffin of the first child she lost. But there were many people comforting her as she said her goodbyes to her infant son. This loss of a child is a universal grief, instantly recognisable, instantly understood. The pain and separation we feel, along with the knowledge that we eventually have to let them go and move on with our lives, adds to our heartache. Edward has watched his family grow, watched the games his brothers and sisters played, heard their laughter and fun they shared together. Yet, although he did not play among them, he knows that one day they will all be reunited with him. He gave me the words of a poem to write down and give to his mother, who still carries his loss in her heart.

MAM

I am here in heaven
with my daddy and friends.
I died when I was little
and we never became friends.
He carried my coffin
on the back of his bike
I became a little angel
to carry the might.
Now I am grown,
I've become a man,
I walk with my daddy
in God's green land.
We have great conversations
Daddy and me.
We are always looking down
and looking after thee.

My brothers and sisters
have families of their own,
my nieces and nephews
are all nearly grown.
I have been watching them grow
each and every day
my brothers and sisters, with whom I never got to play.
But if I could go back for just a second or two
I'd give my mam a great big kiss and a hug or two.
But always remember and never forget
I am a shining light that lives with the best.

Through my interaction with my angels I have become increasingly convinced that our lost children are never far from us. I was visiting a dormer bungalow once and as I got out of my car and walked towards the entrance, I saw a young boy looking down at me from the centre window in the dormer section. As soon as I entered the house, I noticed a man sitting in a chair. He was elderly and he had a pronounced and disfiguring curvature on his spine. He disappeared in a flash. I am so used to these sudden apparitions and tend to take them in my stride. I know that sooner or later I will understand their significance. Jessica, the woman who had invited me to her house, welcomed me and introduced her two young daughters. I mentioned the elderly man with the hump on his back who I had seen sitting in her kitchen. She recognised him. He had lived nearby and was a regular visitor to her house until his death some months previously.

When the little boy at the window showed no sign of appearing, I asked Jessica where her son was. She became very still. A wave of grief passed over her face. Before she told me, I had guessed that her son was dead and his spirit had been staring down at me from the window.

She nodded when I described him and became quite emotional when I told her his name. She admitted that she was always conscious of his presence when she entered that room, even though he had died when they lived in a difference house. Because of this, she had believed the sensation of kinship and love she experienced was her imagination. I assured her that he was present in her life and only a gentle breath separated them.

These beautiful souls can teach us so much about forgiveness, about laughter, about the beautiful light that opens up to a world that holds the key to our existence.

12

Grounding and Releasing

Is this journey with my angels helping me to understand
that I walk each day in a divine light? Is it taking me back
to a place I have forgotten but is stored in a memory within me?
Must I leave behind all the physical attributes my
physical body has stored so that my light body can
come closer to me? In order to do so, must I surrender all
that I know and find a new way?

IN CHAPTER 3, I MENTIONED TWO PARTICULAR exercises that are essential in my work – grounding and releasing – and I'd like to share them with you.

Grounding helps us to come into the moment, to align our physical, emotional and well-being together. Through regular practice, we become more focused and balanced. If we can free our mind for a short while each day, we will learn to sit in stillness and be aware of the subtle energies created by our angels and spirit guides when they surround us. Angels do not have physical bodies and operate on a different vibrational level to us. In order for them to communicate with us, they have to lower their vibrations so that we may hear their guidance.

When we allow ourselves to tune inwards, we become aware of the many thoughts and emotions we have at that moment. We hear the clamour in our mind, the conflicting demands for attention. This is our ego, that little voice that communicates with us, that little voice that tells us we are no good, that we will never accomplish anything worthwhile in our lives. All is doomed, all we touch ends in failure. That negative block will always prevent us from reaching our full potential. It is essential to let it go and learn to take our lives in a more positive and meaningful direction.

Communicating with angels is one of the most beautiful things we can do. But in order for our angels to come closer, we must learn to let go of our ordinary state of mind, the mind that is concerned with the negative things. Through grounding, we will learn to cast off those unnecessary thoughts and concentrate on what is important – to sit in tranquillity and listen for the voice within us that is always reaching out to help us.

Grounding does not have to be a long-drawn-out exercise, it can be done in a few minutes. This practice belongs to everyone, those with spiritual and religious beliefs and those who are non-faith.

Exercise for Grounding

Angels view the rainbow as a bridge between our two worlds. We use it to focus our energies on its luminous symbolism. Within this exercise, we will create a rainbow that will anchor and centre us. It will help us to take our awareness into the moment.

Find a quiet place where you will not be disturbed. Sit quietly, take a deep breath and close your eyes. Imagine that there is a powerful white light coming from the soles of your feet. It begins to connect you to the earth below. Now visualise a beautiful rainbow beginning to travel up through mother earth. Watch as it travels all the way towards the tops of your toes. Feel the energy from this rainbow as it begins to surround you, see the colours illuminate around you. Now see this rainbow begin to travel up over your feet, up over your legs, over your thighs. See the rainbow travelling over your lower back, travelling deep down into the base of your spine, feel the energies from the rainbow as it begins to earth you more and more. Now watch as this rainbow travels over your hips into your stomach, travelling all the way into your chest. Feel the light from this rainbow penetrate your whole being and begin to take away any negativity, pain or trauma you may be carrying.

See this rainbow travelling towards your heart, feel its love travelling deep down into the centre of your heart, carrying a love that is totally unconditional, a love that will remain with you forever. The rainbow now begins to travel up over your fingers and hands – see it travelling up over your arms, your neck and shoulders. As it travels, it continues to remove any negativity that still lingers within you. See it travel over your throat and face, over your forehead until it reaches the top of your head. You are now beginning to feel totally relaxed and safe as this rainbow circles around you, grounding you into the moment when you are ready to communicate with your angels and spirit guides.

Exercise for Releasing

Before you begin this exercise, you will need a pen and paper.

Sit, relax, take a deep breath and close your eyes. Mentally say to yourself, 'I now release everything that is blocking me from hearing the voices of my angels.'

Repeat this three times. As you focus on doing this, you may find emotions beginning to surface. You may carry a lot of anger, fear, envy, jealousy, resentment, self-worthlessness. Whatever these emotions are, just let them surface. Do not be afraid of anything. Even if you do not understand your feelings, just allow them to be there. Sometimes you will be surprised at what comes to the surface. They may be issues that you need to look at in your life and that's okay. Let them come.

When you are finished, open your eyes, take your pen

and paper and write down everything you experienced. Then take a few minutes to share them with your angel. Always remember that angels love you. They have a deep understanding of your needs so never be afraid to talk to them. They do not mind how much you ask for their assistance. As you share, you will come to know your angel in a beautiful way. You will begin to form a bond of friendship that will take you to a place where those channels of communication will become stronger and more trusting. So open up those channels. Open up like a beautiful butterfly. Step out and be that beautiful person. Be secure in the knowledge that your angel walks with you every step of the way.

Spontaneous Writing

Another exercise I have found useful, particularly if I am troubled by some issue, is to write freely for a short period each day, or whenever I have a free opportunity. This is a more spontaneous mental workout and not as focused as the Releasing exercise. It is designed to develop the creative drive within you that is all too often buried under the pressures of a busy lifestyle. You need spend no longer than ten minutes writing, unless you discover that you have struck a creative spark – in which case, run with it.

Writing down your thoughts and feelings is a powerful tool that helps you to have a clearer understanding of the worries that can preoccupy you and deplete your energy. Spontaneous writing is like confiding in a trusted friend except that you are the only person who will see what you write. You do not even have to read it back to yourself if you don't want to. But by that physical act of writing, your mind is forced to slow down. Your thoughts settle, instead of running ahead of you or circling like tireless mice on a thread wheel. As you transfer your thoughts onto paper, they develop a different energy, even a different perspective. You can indulge yourself as much as you wish, be as outrageous or as awful as your wish. This is your space and you are physically unblocking any negativity that is controlling you. Your writing is free from scrutiny, free from expectations, free from judgement.

Quite often, if you take an issue that has been bothering you for some time and explore it through this form of spontaneous writing, another opinion can emerge. One you never considered, despite the fact that this issue has taken over your mind. This new perspective can surprise you. You wonder how that idea suddenly emerged and transferred itself to paper. But it was within you all the time, buried deep under your main preoccupations. By exploring it, you can end up with a totally different viewpoint, hopefully one that is constructive and helpful.

At the end of the exercise, you can tear up your pages, burn them, scatter them, or carefully store them in a private place. They have served their purpose. Even if you have only written a few words that seem meaningless, the time you spent writing them has released your mind, relaxed your body. Through your spontaneous writing, you may have unearthed a little gem of wisdom, a nugget that gives you an insight into life and its many complexities.

13

Echoes Across the Divine Bridge

Everything about my journey inspires me to find
the deeper levels of a world that I have come
to love and understand. To believe that the power
within me answers the call of an angel.
I am everything this world has given me, yet it
reaches out to show me more.
It is far from over. It is only the beginning.

MAKING NEW FRIENDS HAS ALWAYS BEEN important to me and, in Spain, I developed one of the most important friendships of my life. Anne and Jan are a Norwegian couple who settled in Spain and lived for a time around the corner from us. Jan is a healer and this has added another dimension to our relationship. This is a warm and supportive friendship but, looking back over the event that drew us together, it is impossible to believe our relationship would have developed without the intervention of angel power.

But I will let Anne tell you her story:

My father passed away on the 5 August 2001 and it was the following spring when Francesca and her husband, Fran, visited Spain on a holiday. We lived just round the corner from their house and they knocked on our door one afternoon. Francesca said she might have a message to me. She asked if I knew a man who had a habit of doing something with his mouth.

I said I didn't, but she asked again.

'Do you know a man who flicks his mouth with his fingers and makes a little sound, like ticks … ticks … ticks.'

I still said no, but then my husband elbowed me and said, 'That is your father.'

I think I had known it was him when Francesca described that little mannerism, but I was a bit scared of the whole thing!

She said she had only called to tell me that it was my father. She told me not to be afraid.

Yeah, right! It was my father, who passed in August. How do I believe in that?

The next morning Francesca knocked at our door again. 'Your father and I have had a conversation this morning,' she said. 'He wanted my attention, and was using his stick to tell me he wanted his daughter to know he is with her all the time.'

Well, I was still a bit scared of this situation. But it was a great thought that he was with me.

The next time we saw 'the Irish couple' was in autumn of the same year. We had moved to another town and we drove down to Orihuela Costa to meet them.

Francesca and Fran had brought some friends from Ireland with them, a lovely young couple from Dublin. One evening, we all went to a restaurant for supper. We were all seated around the table. Francesca was sitting next to me, and suddenly she put her fingers up to her ear, and told me she has 'a man here that you know'.

It was not so scary this time … just exiting!

'Do you know an old pocket watch?' she asked.

'Yes, I do,' I answered.

'Do you know an old purse?' she asked.

Again I replied, 'Yes, I do.'

'It has some old papers in it,' she said.

'I am not sure about that,' I replied.

'There is a ring there,' Francesca said. 'It is not worth much money, but it means a lot to your father.'

'I know about the ring, it belonged to my grandmother, my father's mother,' I told her.

'Where is the ring now?' Francesca asked.

'I am not sure, but …' Then Francesca interrupted me and said, 'It is your brother who got the ring.'

I texted him at once. The message came back, 'The ring is here.' A man of few words, my brother.

'Who has a celebration coming up?' Francesca asked.

'It is my mother,' I replied. 'She will be seventy years this December.'

'Your father wants you to give your mama a bottle of champagne,' Francesca said.

I was not sure if my mother liked champagne at all. A small bottle would do, so that was what I bought her.

Francesca wrote down on a napkin all the things she told me at that dinner. I saved it for the next time I was going to Norway to visit my mother. This happened some months later. I spent an evening with my twin sister, my brother and my mother. We were sitting in the living room drinking coffee when suddenly my mother asked, 'What was all that about your father and the things happening when you were having dinner with Fran and Francesca. Maybe you will tell us about it now?'

I had the napkin with me, and started to tell it all.

Then my mother came with the old pocket watch. 'This belonged to your father, and your youngest sister. A neighbour damaged it when you were just small kids,' she told us.

The purse was the next thing she brought us. And in that purse it was two slips of paper. It was old paper money, which was not valid anymore.

Then I told them about the ring. And my brother showed it to us.

'What does this mean?' my mother asked.

'It is just to tell us all that he is with us,' I said.

Two seconds later my twin sister said, 'Someone just hit me gently at my cheek.'

'Me too!' said my brother.

My brother is grounded. He did not believe these things, at least this is what he said.

'Do you understand?' I repeated. *'Our father is just telling us that he is here!'*

That evening, when we had dinner with Anne and Jan, we cried and we laughed together. This happens regularly when readings become emotional. Thankfully, I also laugh a lot when I am in communication with my angels as they have the most wonderful sense of humour.

Our friendship with Anne and Jan continued to grow. After I had moved permanently to Spain, Fran and I made our first trip to their native country. They had many contacts in Norway and, on two occasions, Fran and I have been invited to do readings and run a series of successful angel evenings. Language is not a barrier as most people we meet have excellent English. The first time I accepted the invitation to visit Norway, I was somewhat apprehensive. This experience would bring me outside my comfort zone. Would the knowledge I had gained through my communication with my angels be sufficient to convince the people I would meet that I was bringing genuine messages and advice to them? I released any uncertainty and saw it as another challenge to overcome.

The welcome and warmth of the Norwegian people overwhelmed me. But the most striking feature was the sense of belonging I experienced when I arrived in Hønefoss. The belief that I had once lived there became even stronger as I was driven towards Javnaker where I would be conducting my work. This intense sensation of belonging, of being at ease in familiar surroundings, was not accompanied by flashbacks or memory triggers, at least not then. But at one point, as we passed a group of houses, my sense of connection was so strong that I believed I could pick out the house where I'd lived in this previous life. I arrived at the health centre where the atmosphere was so calm and embracing that I felt quite emotional. I described the familiarity I was experiencing towards my surroundings to the woman who had escorted me there.

'I feel as if I've come home,' I said.

Another woman was sitting quietly in the background. I did not notice her until she spoke. 'You *have* come home,' she said. 'Trust your reaction.'

Perhaps she was right. The impression stayed with me throughout the visit and added greatly to my enjoyment. On both trips, I met wonderful people and enjoyed learning about a different culture. But the problems I encountered from the people who came to me for readings were the same in Norway as anywhere else. People in pain from an unresolved past, from hurt inflicted on them by people they loved and trusted. People suffering from a lack of confidence in their ability to influence change in their lives. Their desire to stay with the unhappiness they know rather than risk an uncertain future. And always, the longing to know that a loved one is happy in that other world beyond our vision.

The work I do with my angels is often subjected to scepticism. I have no problem with other people's views. People are entitled to their opinions just as I am entitled to my belief in my angels. But I've discovered that even the most sceptical person longs for some reassurance that life does not end with the last, slow breath. I meet them constantly. The people who say, 'I'm a sceptic. Life ends with death. There is no tomorrow in the so-called spirit world but just in case … just in case …'

I can almost touch their hunger when they hand me a photograph and say, 'Can you tell me anything about this person?'

I met Ingrid, a warm-hearted, friendly woman, on my most recent trip to Norway. Fran and I had been invited to spend the weekend together in her picturesque holiday home on an island in one of Norway's many stunning fjords. The icy splendour of the scenery took my breath away and I was instantly at home on this peaceful island. Ingrid offered us tremendous hospitality in her home but admitted when we met for the first time that she had no belief in a world she could not touch – or in the angels who guide me through it.

I had been working hard all week and was glad to rest from the concentration needed for my angel readings. To be honest, when Ingrid confessed that she was sceptical about my work, I was rather relieved. It meant I could relax my mind and focus on exploring my rugged surroundings. But before the weekend was over, Ingrid produced an old-fashioned, sepia-tinted photograph of a man and woman, and asked if I could read anything from it.

I reminded her that she was a sceptic and my angels, as

well as myself, were off-duty. However, she persisted and I was gradually drawn towards this photograph. I sensed that the people in it had once had a strong connection to the island. She told me they were her great-grandparents and that they had built this beautiful wooden house as their holiday home.

Almost as soon as I focused on the photograph, I became aware of a young man. He was not in the photograph but I could see him clearly in my mind's eye. I understood that he also had once had a deep connection to this island. I could also tell that he had died young and tragically. From my description, Ingrid recognised her uncle, who had indeed died when he was a young man. He had spent many holidays on the island and loved visiting it. Ingrid only had a vague memory of him. She was a child when he passed away, but she remembered his death and the sadness this caused within her family.

I could tell that this young man was burdened by something but it was unclear what exactly was upsetting him. This burden he carried was connected, yet not connected, to the island. It turned out that he had had a young girlfriend who was broken-hearted after his death. She had drowned a short while later, but her death had not occurred on the island.

I asked Ingrid if this young woman had taken her own life. Could this be the reason for the grief this young man was transmitting to me? Ingrid shook her head. She, along with everyone else who knew the tragic circumstances, had no idea if his girlfriend's death had been accidental or deliberate. I could only hope that beyond the veil that separates us from this life and the next, this young couple are united and happy together. The answers to such mysteries are not always revealed to me but Ingrid, my sceptical hostess, admitted that she has always felt the presence of someone watching over her on the island. She had wondered if it was her uncle or, perhaps, her grandparents. I was able to tell her that it was this young man.

He watches over her when she comes alone to the island, as she often does. Being alone does not bother or frighten her, as she loves this wonderful retreat, with its bracing air and majestic fjord. He told me that he loves to listen to her singing. Ingrid is a singer and always gives voice when she is alone on the island with no one to interrupt or disturb her.

She described how, on one occasion, she arrived on the island late at night. She was tired from the trip and, after lighting candles around the living room, she lay down on the sofa with a blanket over her. She drifted off to sleep but woke when someone shook her shoulder. The shaking was so persistent that she flung off the blanket and sat up. As she did so she realised that the candles had burned down and the wax was blazing. A fire could easily have started and Ingrid was convinced that this presence she had often sensed around her had saved her life. I agreed with her.

By then all thoughts of an angel-free weekend had disappeared as Ingrid was intent on finding out if there were other souls lingering among the timbers of this old wooden house. A young girl in her early teens manifested. She was holding a toy carousel and she had the appearance of a sad child. I knew that she had grown into a sad adult. Ingrid believed she was the soul of an aunt who once lived in solitude in Ingrid's family home. She had only known her aunt as a private, reclusive woman but she remembered seeing the toy carousel in her room.

What I experience are glimpses. Gentle whispers of lives once lived. I do not probe any further. Otherwise, I would be submerged under the weight of history. The information I receive from a soul who pauses to convey a message to me will usually be accompanied by some symbolic sign that the living person will recognise as proof of their presence. This was the case with the carousel. This old house had one last spirit to reveal before I left. The man I saw was riding a bicycle. He repeatedly called out a name and I heard it distinctly. Lillian … Lillian … Lillian. Ingrid's partner recognised his mother's name and also acknowledged the presence of his father, who had been a keen cyclist in his lifetime. The message from his father was that although Lillian, who had been his wife on this earth, was ill, he was watching over her.

14
Healing with the Angels

My angels are radiant with the source of love.
Our lives flow in harmony. Each day is filled with blessings.
I walk with peace in my heart.
They have embraced me with their healing light.

ANGELS ASSIST US IN ALL AREAS, ESPECIALLY WHEN we need healing. Our illnesses may not be life-threatening or need medical assistance, but they can manifest within our system in many ways, particularly if we are coping with stress, fears or injustices, imagined or real. We may need healing around love, forgiveness, abandonment, hatred, past pain and trust, loneliness, isolation, jealousy and envy. It is easy to be self-critical. Self-worth demands a tougher strategy and we may be troubled by low self-esteem. We may be carrying baggage from the past. Whatever is bothering us, we are surrounded by wonderful angels and spirit guides who offer us their assistance as we begin to heal.

Sometimes we need to look at the different stages in our lives, from childhood to adolescence, early adulthood and at the person we have become. At each stage, we may hold on to various issues, memories, habits and patterns, and the reasons why we cling to negativity can be buried deep within us. In order to begin the healing process we need to look at these reasons. This can be a time of great pain when we are asked to go beneath the surface of our lives and slowly bring to mind whatever is causing difficulties in our lives. No one likes to go back and remember unpleasant times, but it may be necessary to open up those old wounds if we are to move forward.

When we begin to heal, there will always be a higher power helping us to cope. Each of us has a healing angel assigned to us. It is up to us to welcome them. If you are not sure they are there and do not know how to call them, you can ask your guardian angel to guide them to you. When you become aware of their presence, talk to them. We must tell them where we need healing the most. Let them begin the healing process but remember that nothing is ever accomplished overnight.

They will guide us to different aspects of healing. They may encourage us to seek the help of doctors, counsellors or healers – or instruct us in the methods we need in the area of self-healing. Our first step is to be honest with ourselves. When we embark on this road to healing, we begin to see things from a different perspective. Greater clarity enters our lives. We become happier, more at peace with ourselves. As we begin to relax, we experience great changes within and around us. When we learn to forgive, we begin to release all the anger, hatred, jealousy and envy we have been holding. This brings about remarkable changes in our personality as we become more outgoing and sure of ourselves. This personal development takes us to a place where we begin to love ourselves, and this love will spread to all those around us.

Love, especially self-love, may be very difficult for us. Even saying the words 'I love you' can be too emotional. We should let the angels do this work for us. Each angel has been given special tasks to assist us and each one takes us on a journey of self-fulfilment and growth. Love begins within ourselves. If we cannot love ourselves, how can we love anyone else?

Love is natural. We are born with it. A mother experiences that rush of love when she holds her newborn baby. But for some of us, that bond may not exist. There may be difficulties in a parent's life that causes them to feel unconnected to their child. This can continue until the child becomes an adult with no sense of what it is like to be loved. This pattern can continue until we decide that we deserve to be loved. Hurtful memories around our childhood may be deeply buried but, from time to time, they will surface as extreme anger and cause us to lash out at the people around us.

Sometimes we hold back on love, maybe through fear of rejection or the belief that it is better to be alone than to share our thoughts and emotions with someone else. There may be times in our lives when we are hurt by the people closest to us who let us down – or seem to take from us continually, yet give nothing back in return. They are never there to support us when we need them and because we are close to them, this hurts even more acutely.

Family breakdowns can occur because of alcohol or drug-related problems, or physical and emotional issues. These major factors make us feel totally alone and isolated, drifting through life without any support or guidance. This causes us to hold on to resentment, anger, frustration and periods of helplessness.

What can we do to take away all of these negative emotions? Do we begin a healing process to help us let go – or do we stay as we are, not knowing to whom or where to turn? To accept the latter is to live a life that is fearful, unhealthy and unbalanced in every way. It allows us to be absorbed in a destructive, negative pattern. There is an alternative. We can go inwards and listen to a power that is greater than ourselves, whose only purpose is to help us to heal. God, our Divine Source, is within us, nothing separates us, and he will be aware of our healing process at all times.

Healing needs a willingness to let go of all that is no longer necessary to our lives. It takes courage to release old memories, to be honest and open with ourselves. I have learned much in the area of healing with my angels. They have taught me the art of linking inwards, so that I listen to the rhythm of my body. My body is a life-force energy that operates on a vibration level greater than my mind. When I tune into that vibration, my body has a wonderful way of sending signals that let me know it is not in harmony with me. When I understood what my angels were showing me, I realised that I could learn to heal my body when anything surfaced that was out of tune with my life. My body is a vehicle that carries me through my life and, as such, must be cared for. I am the only one in charge of me.

Those signals can be very subtle and are not always easy to interpret, as Celine discovered when she came to me for healing. She had been sneezing incessantly for weeks and was very distressed when she showed no signs of stopping, despite having tried the usual remedies.

Usually, when I am doing spiritual healing, I sense the presence of that clear, calming green light around the person who has come for healing. I know then that Archangel Raphael has come to my assistance and he will work with me through Angel Ann.

Angel Ann said the sneezing had occurred because of an inner conflict within Celine. She was full of self-doubts and had serious problems around her own abilities. I asked Celine if this was a true representation of her mood at that particular time. She agreed that it was. Her career was her problem. She believed she was unable to handle her workload and she had become intensely self-critical.

We asked Angel Ann's advice and she told Celine to recite positive affirmations about herself. They would ground her and, over a period of time, change her thought patterns from being a negative to a positive outlook and a belief in herself.

Angel Ann gave me the words of a prayer to Archangel Gabriel which I passed on to Celine. She accepted the affirmation and recited it every day. This ritual became quite significant as it helped her to examine the reasons why she was self-critical. Over a period of time, her new way of thinking brought great change into her life and gave her the courage to start believing in all her own abilities.

Archangel Gabriel

O Archangel Gabriel!
I come to you today to seek the guidance that is within me
Give me the vision of my soul so that I may understand the journey that I take
Give me the courage to reach the many goals and tasks that I set for myself each day
Give me the eyes of my soul so that
I may understand the purification that is in my heart
Give me the wisdom to cleanse my body
So that only the purest of thoughts enter my soul
And as you come close to me, teach me to understand that the power of my thoughts can heal everything that is within me.

Angel Lana
Channelled by Francesca Brown

Affirmations, when recited regularly, calm our minds and help us to focus on what we want to achieve. As we begin to practise our positive thoughts, our conscious mind absorbs those thoughts and takes us into an area where we have the power to heal our self-doubts.

The second person I want to talk about is Trevor, who had been suffering severe shoulder pain for the previous two years. Again, he had tried every remedy, every exercise, without results. When he came, I could see a dull glow manifesting around his shoulders. This was where I decided to work. Angel Ann explained that Trevor's thoughts always centred on the lack of things in his life. His fear of not having enough, of not being good enough and of not being able to support his family. In any situation outside his control, he always considered the worst possible scenario. Even though he had a good life, a wonderful family and a well-paid job, he still felt it was not enough. He always needed more.

Angel Ann told him to appreciate and bless what he possessed. Only then would he believe he had everything he needed. He had to trust in the higher power that was guiding him. If he took the time each day to listen to his inner voice, he would know that he had nothing to fear. Angel Ann gave him a positive affirmation to say and he willingly accepted it.

Some weeks later, he explained to me that the more he said the affirmation, the more his attitude began to change. He accepted the truth that he would always have the ability to provide for himself and his family. In doing so, he began to appreciate everything he had. He felt positive and at ease with himself and, most importantly of all, the pain in his shoulder disappeared. He realised that the tension of his negativity had caused an incessant stress in his physical body. Since then, he has learned to communicate with his angels and also to listen to those signals in his body that help him to heal. The affirmation that the angels gave to him was:

God is the source of my supply. Everything I now need he gives to me, my home, my food, my work, my shelter. There is nothing that God does not do for me.

Simple but effective. While affirmations are powerful tools to help us think positively, I would never look upon them in any way as an alternative to medical treatment. I will always recommend that a client contact their medical practitioner if I have the slightest suspicion that they are carrying a physical illness. Usually, the people who come seek a spiritual healing have already tried the conventional approach without any success.

Some time ago, a friend of mine called me and complained of a sore throat. His back was also giving him trouble. When I visited him, he looked like a man of ninety, although he was only in his early fifties. He was withered and hardly able to get out of his chair. Fran and I helped him to lie down and I agreed to do a healing.

As I prepared to start the healing, I asked Angel Ann to guide me to the direct place where I should begin. Usually, healing begins at the person's head and works down through the body. However, I don't work to any specific plan. My approach to each person is different, depending on their needs. As soon as I begin, I can feel cold spots around that area that is blocked. I can best describe this sensation as balls of energy travelling down my arms into my hands, which do not touch the person's body.

In this case, Angel Ann told me to begin the healing at his feet. I moved my hands over that area and the sensation was intense, like ice meeting the heat of my palms. Angel Ann told me that my friend had manifested this illness. It had started with a sore throat and then travelled down his back to his feet. She kept mentioning the word 'support'. I asked my friend if that word meant anything to him and he said it made perfect sense.

We did a healing for a couple of days and he started to recover. There had been a split in his family and he had separated from his wife and children for a period of time. This was not through anyone's fault, but had occurred because of certain unavoidable circumstances. As a result, he was unable to offer them the support he believed they needed. His way of coping was to become ill. He was not pretending or malingering. His symptoms were real and causing him deep distress. Once he had a clearer understanding of how his emotions were affected by this parting, he was able to recover.

Sometimes it is easier to be sick than to deal with reality. I remember working with a man who had many difficulties in his life. Angel Ann agreed to work with him but she said he needed more psychological assistance. He was reluctant to visit a counsellor. In fact, he was quite adamant that he was not prepared to take that route. I agreed to work with him for a few weeks in the hope that he would feel confident enough to seek that specialist help. On the fifth visit, he told me he had booked a counsellor. I had done what I could do – and I was delighted that my assistance had helped to bring him to the next level.

I am not trained in counselling and I am extremely careful about what I say to people. If people are on medication, I would never advise them to stop, even if they ask my opinion. I work on a different level and it is the intercession of my angels that guides me.

A woman once asked me to see her son. Before John arrived, I felt very agitated and restless. When I asked Angel Ann why I was so disturbed, she told me that John suffered from schizophrenia. This shocked and also worried me. I asked Angel Ann if I should go ahead with the reading and she replied, 'Why not? He is no different from anyone else.'

John was on medication and was a lovely young man. But he needed the type of professional help that I could not possibly provide. When I was reading for him, I felt as if I was lost in my own head. The restlessness continued the whole time he was with me. Instead of being relaxed in my chair, as I usually am, I wanted to pace up and down the room. I could not get my thoughts together.

Angel Ann told me to relax. 'These are not your symptoms,' she told me. 'But as soon as you make that connection all those symptoms will disappear.' It was exactly as she said. Once I acknowledged the symptoms, they disappeared.

Having my mind invaded by someone else's symptoms can also happen when I am communicating with the spirit world. When someone has passed on, who had been suffering from Alzheimer's in the final stages of life, wishes to communicate with a loved one, my mind becomes hazy. I'm unable to think straight and have no sense of where I am. I've learned to recognise these symptoms. I will ask the person who is attending the reading if the person trying to make contact with them died from Alzheimer's. As soon as they tell me that this is the case, the symptoms disappear. I don't believe the person who suffered so tragically has carried that dreadful disease into their world of light, but by manifesting itself through me, it helps their loved one on this side validate their presence.

On one occasion, I was reading for a man when the spirit of his brother came in. I felt physically sick. The pain that shot through my liver and my kidneys was unbelievable. I asked this man if his brother had died from kidney failure. He said he had. As soon as he acknowledged this fact, the symptoms vanished. In the beginning, I was frightened every time this happened, but Angel Ann persuaded me that I would not be harmed by such physical manifestations.

I now look upon such indicators as a gift, a validation, an acknowledgement from my angels that when we open ourselves to angelic influences, everything is revealed to us.

15
Bringing Tidings of Comfort

I know within my heart that the bonds of love never die
between the physical world and the spiritual world.
There is nothing that constricts us, no ocean or mountain.
There is no desert to cross. The power of love that is stronger
than anything we know will break through all of those
boundaries to reveal their message to us.

ON A SNOWY MORNING IN WINTER WHEN I WAS
convinced no one would come out and face the elements, I
heard a car drawing up outside. I was booked to do a series of
readings that day and this was my first client. I was working
for a week from a cottage in northeastern Ireland and the bay
window of the living room where I would do the readings
overlooked the front garden. When I glanced out, I saw a man
standing in the garden with a cigarette in his hand. He was
wearing a blue anorak and, for some reason, the blue shade
seemed to fill my eyes. I felt uncomfortable with the idea

of someone being so close to me. I needed privacy for both myself and the woman who had booked her appointment. I decided to pull over the curtains. As I walked towards the window the man disappeared. A wind suddenly stirred in the room. The air chilled. I realised then that this was not a natural occurrence.

When the woman entered I asked, 'Do you have any connection to a man with a blue anorak, who smokes?' As I continued to describe the man, her surprise turned to astonishment. 'That is my husband you are talking about,' she said.

He had died some months previously and she was heartbroken over her loss. She began to cry and I, as happens on many such occasions, cried with her. Such manifestations can awaken strong emotional responses in me as well as in the person who recognises the presence of the departed soul. This woman's husband gave her the most wonderful messages. She was able to affirm everything he told her. He did not appear again, but for the whole time we were together in that centrally heated room we were both aware of the coldness surrounding us.

I was reminded of that spiritual encounter when two women made an appointment to see me together. They had different surnames and I'd no idea how they were connected to each other. The name of the woman who had the first appointment was Laura. I was preparing myself mentally to receive her when

I became conscious of a strong energy playing over me. I heard a male voice saying, 'Elizabeth. Not Laura.' This message was repeated a few times. I knew I had to pay attention to it.

When the two women arrived, I asked them if they were related and discovered they were mother and daughter.

'I've heard the voice of a gentleman and he keeps telling me to read to Elizabeth first. Does that make any sense to you?' I asked.

The older woman said, 'I'm Elizabeth.'

I said, 'This is your husband and he's only passed over about five or six months ago.'

She agreed that that was what had happened. I then repeated that he was anxious to communicate with her first.

Her daughter readily agreed and during the reading, he had many wonderful messages to say to his wife. I could see him standing in a beautiful garden.

'He's taken me into a wonderful garden,' I told her.

She shook her head and told me he never had any time for his garden.

'You're right,' I replied. 'But it's not *his* garden. He's with another man called Steve and they are standing together in Steve's garden.'

Elizabeth immediately realised this was her brother-in-law. Steve had had the most wonderful green fingers and his garden was his pride and joy.

Elizabeth was wearing a thick, woolly jumper and her

husband said, 'Tell her that I know she keeps me close to her heart.'

On hearing this, she reached inside her jumper and pulled out a heart-shaped locket with her beloved husband's photograph inside.

He said, 'Tell her I went with a bang.'

She nodded and said he had always wanted to go suddenly and would say to her, 'When God takes me, I want to go with a bang.'

After Elizabeth's reading ended, Laura came into my room. Her father was still present. He was able to comfort her about some challenging issues that she was trying to handle, and assured her that things would work out for her in the end. But it had been important for him to communicate with his wife first. This is where it is vital that I trust in this other dimension – and to heed the voices of angels when they speak to me. If I had ignored this voice and taken Laura as my first appointment, the readings could have ended disastrously or, at the very least, the communications would have been muddied and confused.

I have become accustomed to sudden manifestations and am no longer startled when they occur. In the course of writing this book, a young girl in her early teens has appeared in my room. She was seated in an armchair and almost in the same instant as I registered her presence she was gone. But she had smiled and I had seen that she had a gap between her front teeth. I also had a strong impression that she loved swimming.

The woman who came for a reading the following day had lost her fourteen-year-old niece. Her death had been sudden and, although this had happened some years previously, the loss was still keenly felt by her family. Her aunt was amazed when I asked if her niece had had a gap between her front teeth. She smiled and admitted that the young girl had been embarrassed by it and never wanted to smile. And she had loved swimming.

Some people go inwards into themselves when such a terrible bereavement happens. Who can blame them? We cannot even begin to imagine the tremendous loss they feel. But this woman had gone outwards. She had suffered and learned how to come to terms with her loss. This awareness had brought her into bereavement counselling in Dublin and the angels were able to confirm that she would help others who are going through a similar painful bereavement.

16

Angels of Manifestation

We are sure and confident in ourselves. We know where
we are going and what we must accomplish to get there.
Our lives flow in harmony. Each day is filled with the
blessings that God gives to us. We are open and compassionate
to all things. We begin to live our lives from a higher perspective,
knowing as we do that we have the ability to create
everything we need for happiness.
We have been touched by an angel.

I'D LIKE TO SHARE WITH YOU A SHORT VISUALISATION
that I carry out with my angels of manifestation. You should
never feel that it is unworthy of you to request help from your
angels, nor must you have any negative thoughts around what
you desire. Your angels are there to help you live your life to its
fullest potential. You must trust in a process that has your best
interests at heart.

The following short exercise is very effective when you

want to make contact with your angels and request their assistance. It is one of my favourite visualisations, where I go into the silence and awareness to connect with my angels and guides. Do not concern yourself with how your request will be received. Let it go. Have faith and trust that your prayers will be answered.

Have a clear indication of what it is you want and write down your intentions. There will be no outside influences, no talking about your request. You will have complete faith in you own ability to understand what is best for you. Always remember that you are guided. Check what you have written down a few times, so that it becomes crystal clear in your mind. This can be anything from peace of mind to a new house. If it is the latter, write down the details of the house and the area where you would like to live. If you are not sure of what it is you require, meditate first on your desires. When it feels right, go with it.

Each day for one month, starting on a particular date that you will decide, go into the silence, into your awareness. Have your list beside you and call on the angels of manifestation. Sit quietly, take a deep breath and close your eyes. Now visualise a team of beautiful angels in front of you. One by one, they will give you a name. Sometimes, this will not happen. Names are of little importance to them but if you feel more comfortable with a name you may ask, and they will oblige you.

Each angel holds a basket in her hand. Watch as one by

one they come towards you. As they do so, welcome them and state your intentions. Place the request into the angel basket. When you have done so, the angel takes the basket with your intentions into the universe. You will visualise each intention as if it has already been received. We can repeat this visualisation with each angel as they approach. When this has been done, we must thank them for coming. It is important to keep our intentions positive at all times during this exercise. The universe has a vast understanding of you and knows exactly what you want and need. As each angel delivers your intention, you must trust, hold faith and believe that the universe has already answered. Now begin to truly believe that you are worthy of everything that you have requested.

I use another positive visualisation, which I call the 'Picture House'.

The picture house can be a joyful place where it is possible to let go of the stresses and strains of everyday life. It is a place where you can create the movie of your life and how you would like to live it. You will use the power of your imagination to create your own reality. Set aside a little time each day for your visualisation work. If you don't see any immediate results, don't let that put you off. It takes time to train our minds into this area of positive visualisation. Stay with it and you will see results. Have faith and trust that everything you require will be given to you – and always remember that the universe has its own way of answering you.

You have the whole cinema to yourself. Buy your ticket and ice-cream, and enjoy the carefree feeling of knowing that this is your time. Take your seat and observe that big silver screen in front of you. Choose your seat and sit down. As you settle, become aware that paper and a pen are to one side of you. On this sheet of paper, list ten things that you feel would make a beneficial difference to your life. These can range from a house, to successful employment, to health and serenity in your life. This list is yours to decide.

On your other side you will find a remote control. If Number Five on your list is a new car, press that number on the remote control. As the movie begins, see yourself in your new car. Observe the make, model and colour. See yourself in it and experience the joy you feel when you drive it.

Do the same for each of your intentions and trust that your angels will help you achieve them. Do not expect a car to be delivered with a card from the angels. Do not expect instant gratification on all your intentions. Just trust in the positivity of your thoughts, the clarity of your goals. Instead of becoming clogged by negativity, exhausted by the feeling that you will never achieve what you want, you will be energised by the belief that everything is possible if your attitude is right. Each day, go to the movies and create the life you truly deserve.

How many times has faith turned our lives around? This faith is your inner voice guiding you to seek your truth and live your life according to you. It is based on an understanding of who you really are. It is a mirror reflection of you at all times. It can open you up to your full potential. It can motivate you to get things done. Reach into your faith, the energy that resides there, trusting that, at all times, it will hold you together.

17

Trusting the Voices of Angels

I listened to my angels and entered the stillness.
It brought me to a place where I found the peace and joy
I needed in my life. I became aware of a voice within my breath.
A voice that was to show me the purpose of my life
and the direction I needed to go.

I AM A MESSENGER. I COULD USE OTHER WORDS – intermediary, mediator, communicator – but 'angel messenger' describes my role in its most simple form. What I have experienced does not belong to the paranormal spectrum, at least not the way Angel Ann has explained it. I've asked her why I was chosen to be an angel messenger. It still remains a mystery to me. She replies that many are chosen but only a few will answer her call.

Three years ago, I met a holy man in Norway. Not that he had any idea of the path that lay before him when he came to me for an angel reading. But I knew by the light that radiated from his presence that I was in the company of someone chosen by angels to be an extraordinary messenger. When I stood up to greet him, I felt as if the room shifted in an indefinable yet palpable movement and he seemed to grow taller before my eyes.

He was a married man with a young family and was caught up in the everyday responsibilities of earning his living. He had some inkling of his special powers, but I knew he did not have a true sense of his own energy or that he was being guided by angels. When I finished his reading, he admitted that he had had a feeling since he was a little boy that he was on a special journey. He had no clear idea of the direction he should take or whether he should develop his skills. To me, he had the most wonderful connection to the world of light and, even though he had come to me for a reading, I felt honoured to be in his company. Angel Ann said his journey would be a slow one. This disappointed me. I wanted to see him develop those wonderful gifts immediately but I understood that it was up to him to either choose or ignore his calling.

Recently, I met him again. As soon as he entered the room, I realised that he had chosen to delay his journey. His light was not as strong. His energy field was low. Yet he was happy with his life. He enjoyed his work, his family. Each day brought its own busy demands. We talked about his last reading when I had seen his light luminous with promise. Now, despite his contentment, I could see that his spirit was striving to begin that journey. It will happen in time – and his presence will influence many lives – but Angel Ann is right, it will be a slow process and will only take place when he is ready to absorb the glorious message that awaits him.

It took a debilitating illness to start me on the journey I was always destined to take. Only when I was laid low, virtually helpless and unable to see a future before me, did I become receptive to this wonderful gift. People sometimes ask what would happen if I belonged to a different culture or faith. Would I still see angels? Perhaps, in that case, there would be a different divine manifestation but the question is irrelevant. I do not over-analyse my experience. It is personal to me, my own individual journey that began when an angel came to my bedside and promised to heal me. In return I placed my absolute trust in her presence and in the host of angels surrounding her.

As a result, I was granted the gifts of visualising the past, present and future. I was encouraged to develop my spiritual healing skills and discovered that I was a receptive channel when voices came to me from the world of light. I don't evangelise or impose my beliefs on others. If someone seeks a reading, it is their own choice to come and hear what the angels have to say. If they attend an angel evening, it is their decision to open themselves to the voices from beyond who come to us with messages of comfort and love. But I cannot change a person's destiny. All I can do is pass on the advice that comes to me through Angel Ann.

A woman, who admitted to being a sceptic, read *My Whispering Angels* and, as a result, attended an angel evening out of curiosity. Although I never spoke directly to her during the demonstration, she came to me when it was over and told me she had been impressed by the specific information I had given to people. She believed I was linking into a strong and positive force, but her jury was still out as regards the existence of my angels. Recently, she emailed me and said she had opened a little door into the realm of angels. I have advised her to go with it and contact me if she needs any help. But for each person, this is their individual journey and I do not interfere.

When we read a book, we become part of that story. We focus on the voice that resonates with us and reflects our own experiences. At times, it seems as if a friend is speaking directly to us from the pages. Many people have contacted me to tell me that *My Whispering Angels* proved to be a great motivational tool that helped them to move forward in their lives and make decisions they had been postponing for one reason or another.

My book would never have been written without the angels to guide me. We live in a clamorous world. Information is constant. Twenty-four-hour rolling news, instant messaging – the breadth of the social networking media widens all the time. The voices of angels are difficult to hear and yet there is an ever-growing awareness of their power. My book, and others dedicated to angels, topped the bestseller list because people want to reach from the clamour into the stillness and seek what is meaningful in their lives.

Shortly after its publication, when Fran and I had returned to Spain, a man knocked on my door with a copy of *My Whispering Angels* in his hand.

'I'm not here for a reading,' he said. 'All I want to say is thank you. I haven't cried for over twenty years. I've had a lot of difficult stuff going on in my life, but when I read your book, my tears could not stop. It was a healing experience.'

He had issues from his childhood that he had never been able to discuss with his wife. But through the voices of the angels that echoed back to him from the pages, he found the courage to open up the hurting part of himself that he had kept under wraps for so long.

One woman, who was in an extremely difficult relationship, told me that reading *My Whispering Angels* forced her to face the reality of her own life. She had gone down many avenues in an effort to save her marriage. Now she could no longer live in denial about what this relationship was doing to her sense of herself as a person, apart from the obvious threat it posed for her personal safety. She said the angels had given her great courage and *My Whispering Angels* had become her bible.

'I know there is help and support out there for me if I take the courage to change my life,' she said. 'I'm now ready to take that step.'

Another woman, whom I'll call Claire, came to see me recently. She had been with me three years previously and, although I vaguely remembered her face, I had no recollection of what we had discussed during her reading. I had no sooner started this reading when I heard Angel Ann's voice telling me that Claire was still in the same abusive marriage. I asked Claire if this was the case and she agreed. The flaws and the danger that lay within that relationship had been exposed in painful detail at the previous reading and she had left me that day determined to end her marriage. Although she had made some effort to achieve a little bit of independence since then, she remained in the same cycle of abuse. I could see that she was desperately anxious to leave her husband, but she believed the time was not right for her to strike out on her own. I could also see that there would never be a right time. But I would never advise anyone to pack their bags and go. All I can offer is a reflection of their lives, as relayed to me by Angel Ann.

However, there are exceptions to every rule. Occasionally, when there is extreme violence in a relationship, Angel Ann will advise a more direct form of action.

'You've got to get out of this dangerous situation,' I told one woman who came to me with desperation in her eyes.

She was a battered housewife whose husband was a successful businessman with an impeccable reputation. A typical pillar of society, but a destructive and brutal man in the privacy of his home. She had done everything she could to save her marriage but, from the outset of the reading, Angel Ann began to reveal the most horrendous stories about the treatment meted out to this unfortunate woman by her husband. They were so personal and distressing that I felt that I could not relate them back to her. But she insisted on hearing what the angels had to say. When the reading ended, and on the advice of Angel Ann, I looked through a telephone directory and gave her the number of a women's refuge centre. With the help of experienced counsellors, this woman was able to escape from her violent relationship. But such personal involvement from the angels is unusual. Free will is what they preach and I, as the messenger, must stand back and allow life to take its course.

18

Positive Consciousness

I am powerful. I have the ability to change all that is within me.
I will not look back in sadness, anger or disappointment,
believing that everything I did was wrong.
I will grow from strength to strength and allow
for new beginnings, new growth.
Channelled by Angel Lana

ANGEL LANA FIRST CAME TO ME AFTER I HAD settled in Spain. She was accompanied by Rebecca, another angel who, like Lana, had a delightful soft energy around her. They brought humour and merriment with them – and a reminder that we must not take life too seriously. Grab the opportunity when it comes to dance and sing and be uplifted. But these angels also have a serious mission and their energy is centred around positivity and creativity. They encourage us to raise our energy fields and effect the change we desire in our everyday lives.

Angel Ann does not drop solutions from the sky. But she puts me in touch with the right people. She opens pathways that I didn't know existed. It took so much courage to trust her. Even today, there are occasions when she states certain things that are going to happen, and I find my courage faltering. Have I the confidence to walk a new path, undertake a new experience? If I hesitate to take the step she believes is right for me, Fran, who used to be the great sceptic, will always remind me that Angel Ann has never let us down.

Years ago she said, 'If you take my hand, I will guide you every step of the way. I will not make you a rich woman, but I will give you everything you need to lead a happy and fulfilled life.'

I have surrendered myself to my angels but they have not taken control over my life. I still have my own free will, the ability to make my own decisions, my independence. But I trust them utterly and believe them when they predict that something will happen. I listen to the voice of Angel Ann when she opens doors and invites me to walk through them.

Many people come for an angel reading in the hope that much will be revealed to them. They will have a better understanding of the ills that befall them, the rushes of uncertainty and depression that can lay them low, the confusion and loss of control that often besets their days. And some come simply to receive affirmation that a decision they want to make is the right one. Like the young girl who came for a reading and nodded when Angel Ann said, 'At home you have a form that you need to fill out for a teaching course. Why are you thinking about it? Go for it.'

I asked the young girl if that information meant anything to her and she said it absolutely did. She had not come for a reading about her future but was seeking affirmation about the choice she was considering – and the words of the angel echoed what was in her own heart. People love to hear an affirmation. It reinforces their own beliefs. Our thoughts can often become muddied by uncertainty or over-analysis as we try to decide if we are making the correct decision.

Sometimes people come seeking reassurance and only want a brief message that gives them hope. I remember how, on one occasion, a woman came to see me and Angel Ann simply said, 'Tell this lady that I am not reading for her. My only message is that your heart will go on. Now live your life.'

I asked the woman if she understood the message and she nodded. Her joy was palpable when she told me she had just had a heart transplant. I apologised for not being able to provide any further information but she said, 'That is all I needed to know.' On the way into the reading, she had told her husband that she finally believed she had another chance at life and the words from Angel Ann confirmed her belief.

But some people come with emotional baggage that they have no intention of laying down. They don't want to heal or effect any changes in their lives. It doesn't matter how much information they receive. They will reject it, if it is not what they want to hear. When one very disgruntled young woman came to me for a reading, I could see immediately that she was not prepared to listen to anything Angel Ann had to say. I gave her all the information that was relayed to me and, although she agreed with it, she simply wanted to know whether or not someone was going to enter her life and bring her happiness. She was angry, drifting from place to place, and seemed unable to comprehend the message from Angel Ann that her happiness had to come from within her. Her first step was to recognise her own hostility and challenge it, rather than blaming everyone else for her dissatisfaction.

Problems don't disappear by themselves – or as a result of an angel reading. There are no immediate solutions to anyone's difficulties. All the angels can do is guide us. If we refuse to listen, that is our own free will at work. When I ask Angel Ann why people don't want to heal their lives, she tells me it is because they are not in a particular place in their mind where they are open to such information. As long as this young woman continues to blame someone else for her unhappiness, nothing will change. Someone could enter her life and things will be okay for a month or two. But if that pattern of blame persists, if she refuses to accept self-responsibility or examine the reasons why her life always seems to let her down, she will continue to drift. She will never gain any awareness about why her longing for happiness has failed her once again. Her life will only move on if she opens her mind to the message and develops conscious awareness.

'Conscious awareness' is about exploring areas of good and bad, negative and positive. In my journey with the angels, I have learned to release what I no longer need in this life. That applied to my emotional as well as my physical baggage. The angels helped me to go in a direction where I learned to use my thoughts in a positive and powerful way. This was not an easy process. Like most people, I could go from negative to positive in the space of a few minutes. I had to learn to be patient, to let go of all my conditioning, to allow the angels to take me to a place where my mind became pure and focused. I recited the beautiful affirmations they sent me and took the time to practise some simple exercises. I could not have imagined how these little acts would bring about the most amazing changes in my life.

It is important to watch for the reaction a negative thought stirs within us. When this happens, we should accept it instead of trying to deny or avoid it. Then release it and heal its hurt by replacing it with a positive thought. By refusing to indulge our niggling private voice, by accepting that we alone created this situation by allowing our ego free rein, we are reclaiming our power. Through this process of healing, our damaging thoughts are weakened. They become less demanding, less forceful. We have the power to make our thoughts strong and worthy. Allow them to take us in a constructive direction.

Be in the moment. It is such an easy thing to say. Be in the moment. We experience that sensation when we wait in silence for a minute as a tribute to someone who has died. Those sixty seconds seem to stretch endlessly before us, until the tension breaks with the sound of a human voice. But how often do we find ourselves wondering at the end of the day where all our precious hours went? How often do we reach the end of a car journey with no recollection of what we saw on our journey? Instead of observing our surroundings, enjoying the moment, we were absorbed in our thoughts, fretting over what we had to accomplish at our journey's end.

It is impossible to be aware for every moment of our lives. But we should try to control our time in a constructive way instead of coasting along on half-formed critical observations of ourselves and our surroundings. Far too often our moods are determined by outside influences over which we have no control. The media is a huge influence, and does not always have our best interests at heart. We must listen and be informed but be alert to manipulation, to heedless comments that can plunge us into negativity without realising where the source lay.

When I began to change my own thought process, I had to be realistic and accept that change was not going to come overnight. This meant being disciplined, allowing myself a set time to practise this new way of thinking. I was confident that when the angels surrounded me, they had my best intentions at heart. I had to give them my time and effort in return. I set aside a period each day and began to work on different problem areas such as fear, my self-esteem, my health, my ability to love myself for what I am, now, at this moment.

I followed their instructions and loved every minute I spent working with them. As I followed their guidelines, I could feel something slowly stirring within me. I felt the force of a positive energy flowing towards me. Life became more peaceful and balanced. I felt strong and powerful. No matter what anybody said, I believed in myself more and more. I was capable. I was responsible for me. I was reconditioning myself and allowing my thought system to reflect all areas of my life.

Today, I have learned to live in that place of profound stillness that my angels revealed to me. I believe and trust that all my prayers have been answered and my needs truly met. I fill my mind, body and spirit with positive feelings that help me to create whatever I need at this moment in time. To believe that our thoughts can transform our lives sounds so simple, yet that is how we effect change. When I love myself, I love everything within me. When I am happy and joyful, all beauty radiates from within me. When I look back and dwell on disappointments or unhappiness, I create a negative energy that results in anger and self-criticism. What can we do about the past except learn from it and move forwards in a new direction. Nothing we do, no amount of agonising and angst is going to change what happened then. But we can change what happens now, and trust that positive energy to carry us into the future.

I would like to share some of my affirmations and exercises with you. By doing so, I hope they will help you when you need to release, let go and change. Trust and believe that you are surrounded by many celestial beings of light. Open your heart and let them heighten your perception. Let them support you and guide you towards a happy and fulfilling life.

Affirmation channelled by Angel Lana

I am powerful. I have the ability to change all that is within me. I will not look back in sadness, anger or disappointment, believing that everything I did was wrong. I will grow from strength to strength and allow for new beginnings, new growth.

As a child of God, I now let go, secure in the knowledge that my pathway ahead is illuminated by the light that sustains everything within and around me. My journey is divinely guided. My life flows with the riches of the universe.

Let the universe take my thoughts into an area of positivity where I will create the life I deserve. Everything I undertake will be successful. I am blessed with an understanding of my purpose. I am in the presence of God and through him all fears, worries and wounds are healed. Love, joy, peace and prosperity flow through my being.

I thank God each day for my blessings.

Each exercise should be repeated three times each day.

Mirror Exercises

Sit or stand in front of a mirror. Relax your body. Say the following affirmations:

I am happy. I am free.

All things are beautiful

Within me.

I love [say your name and repeat this line three times]

The beauty of my life

Is the beauty of God

Living within me

Today my life is beautiful and true

Today will be fantastic

And I will be too.

Whatever I want, whatever I need

I only have to ask and it will be given to me.

As I look into the mirror I gladly say

I am beautiful in every way.

I do not have to change or criticise myself

For my mirror now reflects the beautiful reality of me.

I am a wonderful intelligent human being.

I have the ability to change and to let go
Of all I no longer need in my life.

These are the positive statements through which I have learned to live my life. Do not settle for less than you deserve.

19

Other Times Revealed

A wind howls around me as I listen to their voices.
They tell me to hold on. To believe that those signs I need
to guide my way will come. I am lost in that moment.
Lost in that time. The light of God and his angels are by my side,
guiding me in the right direction.

IN *MY WHISPERING ANGELS*, I DESCRIBE AN EXPERIENCE I had on a beach in Normandy. Briefly, I'll recount it again for those who have not read that book and to place in context an encounter I had two years after *My Whispering Angels* was published.

Fran and I had been holidaying on the continent and we decided to stop off at Normandy on our journey home. We wanted to visit the beaches where the D-Day landings had taken place and reflect on that horrific time. Fran had served in the Irish army and has always been interested in military history. As we drove towards Normandy, a light drizzle began to fall. The sky was overcast, yet I was aware of a lightness in the air, a gentle energy that gathered strength as we approached a headland that looked out over Utah Beach, one of the main landing places for the Allied troops on D-Day.

We saw an elderly man wearing a blue beret standing about 100 metres from us. He was facing the beach and seemed to be lost in thought. When he turned around, we noticed that his chest was emblazoned with military medals. He looked at Fran and saluted him. Fran immediately straightened up and saluted him in return.

As he began to walk towards us, we could see his medals more clearly. Fran recognised his rank as that of a colonel. He spoke to us and told us he had been a colonel with the French Resistance during the war and that he was attending a commemoration ceremony with the remaining members of his unit.

As we stood together looking out over Utah Beach, an angel with a blue shimmering energy materialised to my left. He smiled and gestured towards the sky. A screen appeared before my eyes. This can happen whenever a vision materialises and I immediately understood that I was about to witness something powerful.

I could still see the beach and the sky above me. The clouds parted and a shaft of sunlight streamed down onto the beach. As I gazed at the scene, I saw what seemed like hundreds, maybe even more, of small energetic entities, pulsating and glowing with subdued colours, mauve, purple, blue and white. As they shone over the beach and the beachhead, I began to weep. I understood that I had been offered a glimpse of heaven and these were the souls of soldiers who had died on that beach. I could hear their youthful voices speaking, mostly with American and Canadian accents. The colonel put his hand on my shoulder to try and comfort me. We moved along the beachhead and reached some of the bunkers that surrounded the beach. I could not enter them. The energy had changed and I could feel the panic among the young soldiers who had been trapped in those bunkers. As I continued to look out on the beach, I was aware of the ferociousness of the fighting. I could hear the voices of officers, who were obviously in command, urging their troops forwards. I must have been speaking out loud because the colonel turned to Fran.

'Your wife is a brilliant military historian,' he said. 'It's as if she was here during the landings.'

Fran then attempted to explain to him about my relationship with the angels and their ability to show me events from the past and the future. I'm not sure how much the colonel understood, but he grasped my hands. He had tears in his eyes when he kissed me on both cheeks.

The angel materialised again in this iridescent blue light and spoke these words. 'The road to freedom is the road to your heart.'

He then faded into the greyness of that French afternoon.

Two years later, we were travelling from Ireland to Spain. Fran drives a white van and we always travel by ferry. When we arrived in Cherbourg it was the sixty-fifth anniversary of the D-Day landings. The memorial ceremonies were taking place that weekend and we were unable to find accommodation anywhere in the area. We were allowed to park our van in the grounds of the hotel where we usually stay when we break our journey. We know the staff quite well and the following morning they gave us permission to use the shower facilities and freshen up. We entered the restaurant breakfast bar and discovered that the room was full of soldiers. There were old war veterans as well as soldiers of all ages and all nationalities, including some soldiers from Ireland.

During breakfast we fell into conversation with a group of young American pilots from the 37th Airlift 'Blue Tail' Squadron. In the course of the conversation, one of them asked me what I did for a living. I told him I communicated with angels. I half-expected them to scoff at this information, but they accepted it respectfully and questioned me about my work and the communications I receive. They were open to the concept of their guardian angels and showed great interest when I described the encounter with an angel I had experienced on that beach in Normandy. I described the emotions that had raged through me, the fear and horror I sensed, the cries of anguish I'd heard. As I related the words spoken by the angel, 'The road to freedom is the road to your heart,' one of the young pilots said, 'Hold on for a moment. I want to show you something.'

He left the breakfast bar and returned a few minutes later with a large, colourful publication. It was entitled *The Road to Freedom* and was an account of that period of the war. It had been published to commemorate the sixty-fifth anniversary and each page was filled with evocative, tragic and poignant photographs from that period. I saw the bodies of soldiers, young men lying in twisted positions, immortalised forever on camera. But there were other photographs that lifted my heart, young children smiling and waving at the cameras, a shimmer of hope for the future in that war-torn landscape.

'There's your road to freedom,' he said and presented me with the publication as a gift.

This experience of reliving a past event through the prism of an angel has happened often. One afternoon, Fran and I took time off and visited Ardgillan Castle in Skerries. This historic castle consists of two storeys over a basement. On our guided tour, I entered one of the rooms. The air changed. I felt it instantly but before I had time to register what was happening, I was aware of a mist forming before my eyes. This sensation always comes without any warning and once that vaporous shadow appears, my immediate surroundings become indistinct. I am unaware of physical barriers like walls and doors. Within this hazy shadow I saw an elegant, upright woman sitting on one of the chairs. She was dressed in clothes from another century and had such a regal bearing that without even considering what I was doing, I curtsied to her. Fran looked at me in astonishment and asked what I was doing. I described the woman to him and told him her name was Elizabeth Mary. She disappeared as suddenly as she had appeared.

On the way out, I asked one of the staff if an Elizabeth Mary was mentioned in the history of the castle. He told me she was. She had been baptised Mary Elizabeth but had always been known as Elizabeth Mary. I asked why I had automatically curtsied and was told that people had always curtsied when they came into her presence.

The castle had the usual upstairs and downstairs divide. When I entered the servants' quarters I heard music and the voices of children. The atmosphere was lively but hard-working, and I knew that I was tuning into echoes from the past.

I had a similar experience in Dublin Castle, where there is a strong military and political history. I wasn't there on a historical tour, but was on a more mundane trip to pick up a form Fran needed to fill out for his taxi. Again that mist appeared. My surroundings seemed to evaporate. On this occasion, I saw horses and soldiers. I heard the horses snorting and whinnying. I saw soldiers moving about the yard. As occurred in Normandy, all this movement and noise seemed to come from a screen that had appeared before my eyes.

I have to assume that such visions are triggered in certain

places that resonate with a powerful and emotive history. This history has been imprinted on the landscape and even though the people have moved on, their energy still lingers in the ether. Even walking down certain streets can create this release and I never have any warning about when these images will appear. Sometimes, when there are obvious connections between the place and its history, I understand why this has happened, but sometimes, when a vision appears then passes without leaving any answers, I am left wondering at the vast mysterious depths that I have yet to comprehend.

20

The Sphere of Life

Dear Father in heaven, come this day to be with me.
Fill my life with the joy and peace that I have never known.
Take my hand and guide me to the place where all of
my needs will be met. Trust me with your knowledge,
so I will know that the voice I hear within my heart is You.
Fill me with Your love and compassion.
Open those doors that will lead me to fulfilment.
Help me to avoid the wrong roads that fail me each time
I walk along them. Fill my heart with the belief that
You are always part of my life.
Amen.

THE SPHERE OF LIFE IS A HEALING SWORD, created from the colours of the spectrum and designed to help us in our daily lives. It encourages us to release our emotions, pain, anger, frustrations and anxieties. It strengthens our motivation, heightens our senses, sharpens out hearing, our intuition, our psychic abilities and our spiritual awareness. When we combine all the colours of the spectrum, it can have the most profound effect on our bodies. Each colour represents an angel or spiritual guide who helps us in the areas where we feel most in need of healing.

Spectrum Colours

The colours of the spectrum are red, yellow, green, blue, indigo and silver. Angels will make themselves known to you when you visualise the sphere of life.

If you are more comfortable working with one angel then please do so. By forming such a relationship, you are trusting in the sphere of life to understand and meet your needs.

Red is associated with a beautiful angel called Sophia. Angel Sophia helps us to find the balance and harmony in our lives. We can call for her assistance when life becomes tough. When we feel disconnected from our surroundings and those around us. When our problems threaten to overwhelm us and cause us to stray from our pathway. To find our way back, we should call on Angel Sophia to point us in the right direction and restore that essential balance.

Yellow is associated with a protective angel called Angel Carmen. She is our angel of the night and her healing comes to us during our dreams. As she watches over our sleep, she helps us to release our fears, worries and anxieties. She renews us through our slumbers and helps us to find the strength and courage to face the morning. She builds up our self-confidence, our self-esteem and, most of all, encourages us to become strong and independent. Call on her and trust that her healing methods will have a profound effect on your life.

Green is associated with a truly compassionate angel called Angel Aidan. He is an angel of insight and knows our needs even before we ask him. He travels through a beautiful light to help those in need of love. Angel Aidan teaches us that love comes from within us. To love and be loved is our natural state. It fills us with compassion and directs our lives in a positive way. When we learn to love ourselves, then we are inspired to have peace, compassion and love for those we meet on our journey.

But a time may come when the peace and love we desire no longer touches us. Circumstances may bring about difficult changes and cause turmoil in our lives. Our emotions may be all over the place. We may not like ourselves very much, and this isolation of our spirit can cause us to cut ourselves from family and friends. We are not meant to be alone. Love honours everything within us. To keep this balance, seek the assistance of Angel Aidan. He is a dynamic energy who opens us up to the power of love.

Blue is associated with the inspiring Angel Hayley whose communication skills are powerful. He reaches out to inspire those who have great gifts of communication but may hold them back for one reason or another. He helps us to cultivate our creative skills. When you sing, dance, paint, act, give powerful speeches or involve yourself in any area of the arts, remember Angel Hayley and call on his support. He opens doors of opportunities for us so we may step forward and believe in our own abilities. He places imaginative pathways in front of us to enhance our creativity and bring out the best in ourselves. If we need assistance around our creative skills, or feel that we are encountering emotional or physical blocks, we should call on Angel Hayley to help our creative skills to flourish once again.

Indigo is associated with the awakening Angel Mark who helps us to gain a perspective and an understanding of our spiritual gifts. He is there to establish a relationship with our many angel guides so we may seek their specific guidance when we need them. He helps us to understand the purpose in our lives and is the guide who will bring us back to the Source of life that created us. He shows us the beautiful light surrounding us and lets us know that we do not walk alone. We are always in the company of angels.

Silver is the cord of light that connects us to the God force that dwells within us.

All of life is connected by this cord and it enfolds us in a sense of oneness. It helps us to understand that we are on a spiritual journey to discover the true meaning of our existence. We connect to this silver light through daily prayer and meditation, where we find peace, love and a belief that as children of God we will live forever.

A visualisation through the Sphere of Life.

Find a quiet place where you will not be disturbed. To achieve the maximum benefit from this healing it is best to lie down.

Take a deep breath and close your eyes.

Now begin to visualise a powerful white light. As it grows stronger, you realise it is carrying a magnificent sword. Bring your awareness to the handle of the sword. Notice that each side of the handle is formed by glittering stones. Each stone is a different colour. The stone on the right side of the handle is a heavenly blue. The stone on the left is a shimmering emerald green.

Now watch as the sword begins to come towards you.

You are feeling safe and relaxed. Watch as the sword travels towards the top of your head. It enters your head and slowly begins to travel down through your body. As it does so, you become conscious of a light sensation moving through you as the sword gently cuts its way through the organs in your body, removing any emotional blockages that may have built up inside you. You are aware that this sword is guided by healing hands that direct it to the areas of your body that need the most specific healing.

As this sword moves down towards your feet, you feel as if a great weight has been lifted from you. As you continue to relax, watch as the sword travels up over your body once more and stops at each chakra to restore and balance you. As it does this, you feel lighter and lighter. You find a great cleansing beginning to take place within your body. The healing sword continues to travel upwards and circle the top of your head. Watch as the green and blue lights merge and settle over you in a beautiful waterfall of light.

Observe the light as it travels to your feet and slowly circles them before returning to the top of your head and merging again with the sword of light. You are totally relaxed, aware that the sword has begun the healing process that will remove all your doubts and fears.

It has helped you gain an emotional and spiritual balance. You feel a sense of renewal, a sense of harmony and peace, and a belief that the power to heal your negativity lies within you. The sphere of life carries within it the healing hands of God.

21

Prayers and Aspirations

I am guided by God.
He lights my path today and every day
So I may know the way forward.
He holds my hand to enlighten my way.

Amen

'HE HOLDS MY HAND TO ENLIGHTEN MY WAY.'
Was there ever a time I did not believe this simple truth? Yes,
indeed there was, although I find it difficult to believe I was
not always conscious of the abundant flow of compassion that
streams from God. When things used to go wrong in my life,
I never asked for His help. I worked everything out for myself
and, more often than not, I would find myself in turmoil with
no clear sense of direction.

I was conditioned to believe it was wrong to seek God's
help. Other people's needs were more important than mine.
God would not hear me or be bothered by my requests. If He

was aware of my distress, then why didn't He just solve my problems for me without having to ask for His help? Why did He let me stand in the wilderness and refuse to show me the way forward?

But it was not God who was causing the problems. It was the pattern of my own negative thinking. Every time something went wrong, I felt doomed. The usual pattern would start up in my mind and it went something like this: I might have known it wouldn't work out ... it never had a chance ... why was I so stupid as to believe good things could happen to me? ... I'd better move on ... try something else ... but that too will fail ... I don't deserve to succeed ... good luck happens to other people ... and so on ... and so on.

The negative voice is shrill, pitiless and repetitive. It lurks within all of us, waiting for the appropriate opportunity to strike. If we're not blaming ourselves, we have so many other things to blame our misfortunes on: our environment, our childhood, the government, our partner, even God can come in for a good tongue-lashing from time to time. But we can silence that negative inner voice by drowning it out on a wave of positivity and faith.

Faith in our own abilities, in our own belief that we deserve to receive the riches of life. I'm not talking about material possessions. They are necessary, yes, but they are only the tools that help us to exist – and they, alone, will never guarantee happiness. To dream our dreams and create an environment where they can come true, we need self-belief. We need to understand what the force of positive thinking can achieve. It will bring joy into our lives, peace of mind and an abiding happiness. That is how we open our hearts to the abundant flow of the universe. Doors of opportunity will open for us. We will be more able to cope with the difficult times when they occur because we know that God and His angels are standing beside us, holding us, loving us, supporting us.

I was christened a Catholic, but I do not follow the dictates of that religion. A group of nuns who once attended an angel demonstration I gave were shocked when, in the course of my presentation, I mentioned that I did not believe in hell. They asked why I had this belief when it went against the grain of my Catholic faith.

But I cannot believe that God rules by fear. Humans do. I grew up with the belief that if I told a lie and I died in my sleep, I would go straight to hell. Sometimes I was terrified to close my eyes in case I would wake up with flames leaping around me. I cast off hell at an early age and since then have refused to be burdened with the image of a vengeful God. Angel Ann tells me that He welcomes us all home. We are all His children, no matter how damaged we are, or how far away from Him we stray.

I do not attend mass on Sunday but I love going into a Catholic church. I'll light a candle and meditate – and feel a close connection with God during those quiet moments. I accept that everything He does is only for my highest good. I have seen the results of all His guidance. Even when I doubted, He answered, taking me to a place today where I say, 'Dear God, you lead and I will follow.' What beautiful words. They are full of hope, full of understanding for this God whom I have come to know in a profound way. To dwell in His kingdom is to feel worthy of everything He brings to me. I am not separated from Him. Even in my darkest hour, I am always one with Him.

Prayer has been a tremendous source of strength to me. The intonations and rhythms are as wonderful and powerful today as they were in the beginning. Whether we pray aloud or inwardly is not important. What really matters is the sincerity behind the words.

Sometimes, we ask but God does not answer. Why is this? We must accept that what we seek is not always what we need. It might not sustain us for very long. Have faith in the knowledge that God will always choose what is right for us – and that the final outcome will have a powerful impact on our lives.

Our prayers are like the seasons. They change and grow, become strong and steady. But sometimes they are a weak murmur. There will be prayers that no longer serve us. Then, we move to the next level of prayer and on to a greater sense of awareness.

Can prayer move mountains? Symbolically, yes it can.

Sometimes the weight we carry can feel as heavy as a mountain. Prayer helps to lighten our load and gives us hope that we will be able to cast our burden off in time.

Today, prayer is more important than ever, as the pace of life moves ever onwards. Our world is constantly changing, constantly in a state of flux, with all the anxieties that creates. It is important to pause for a moment, to contemplate our inner being, to allow our minds to focus on the here and now, not what went before or will happen in the next ten minutes. But prayer is not a quick-fix solution. We have to respect the act of praying. We are opening up a communication with God, sharing our hopes and fears, our laughter and joy, our sadness and tears. As we open up this line of communication we are defining the purpose of our existence. We are acknowledging that God is in the centre of our lives and it is from this centre that He answers our requests.

Knock and you may enter
Ask and you shall receive.

How many times have I spoken those words? How many times will I speak them again? To make this leap into the totality of faith can be difficult. But once it is made there is no going back. I believe God is listening. I believe He will answer me. Perhaps His answer will not be what I expected, but I will understand His reasons. He has helped me with my children, my work, my finances. When I face a problem, I share it with Him. And when I do so, my fears and worries fall away.

I would like to share some of my prayer affirmations with you.

God is the source of my supply
And everything I need He gives to me
My home and food, my work, my shelter.
There is nothing that God does not do for me.

The healing light of Jesus Christ
Flows within me.
Healing all the organs of my
Mind, body and spirit
So that my thoughts are positive
In everything I do.

The beauty of my life
Is the beauty of God living within me
My life is beautiful and true
And everything about it
Answers to that truth.
Everything I need
I have with me today.

These positive prayer statements have helped me enormously. They were given to me by my angels. They have brought me to an understanding of my own worth and a belief that God listens when I seek His aid. They led me to a place in my consciousness where I firmly believe that prayer is the miracle within me.

22

A Practical Guide to Working with Angels and Spirit Guides

My child, I am the perfect light that talks with you.
I open that veil bridging our two worlds so that we are
never far apart. When you are happy, I am happy.
When you are sad, I do my utmost to lift your spirits.
I am the guidance within you. I spend periods of
contemplation to restore and balance all that is within you.
I gather the knowledge that I share with you,
encouraging you to open up your road of learning.
We are two lights, Francesca,
on a journey to find the God within.
Channelled by Angel Ann

I WAS MEDITATING ONE DAY WHEN I RECEIVED A distinct image of a man holding a book in his hand. He turned the cover of the book towards me so that I could make out the words *A Practical Guide to Working with Angels and Spirit Guides*.

Underneath this title, a number of wise suggestions had been listed. I have been guided to live my life and conduct my work by those simple pointers – and am constantly astonished by how they relate to everyone's life.

Be open and receptive to all that is within you

If I had ignored the first suggestion, I would have allowed the clamour of my life to drown the voices of my angels. I would have allowed the lure of familiarity and comfort to hide their vision.

Nourish who you are and what you are

I now live by this second dictate – and I constantly advise others to do the same. Angels give us their unconditional love, but understand how difficult it can be for us to love ourselves. Genuine self-love is not vanity or pride or self-absorption. To have regard for ourselves, and make our own space in this world, is essential for our well-being. If we cannot love ourselves, then we are fixated on that reality – and our ego is constantly occupied, worrying about our inadequacies. We must strive to be the best we can, to love what we are, and allow that self-love to embrace those around us.

Open your awareness to a greater understanding of all that is around you

It seems like such a simple rule to follow. But how often do we do it? How many times do we come to the end of a journey and have no memory of what we passed on the way? How many times do we walk in beauty yet do not pause to admire a bird in flight, the blossom on a tree, the scent of the awakening earth? How often do our own preoccupations blind us to the pain of others? How often do we pause as we pull back the duvet at the end of the day and wonder where the hours went?

Tune into a universal energy that will sustain
your mind, body and soul

I struggled in the beginning with this concept of a universal energy. How could I tap into it, use it, apply it to my life? If I let go of my conditioned responses, would it provide me with everything I need? But I now accept that this energy is within me and is channelled by my angels. I trust. I receive.

This remains the biggest obstacle for many people and they are often amazed by the trust I place in this universal energy. It is linked to my angels and it has taken years of learning to reach a stage where I have absolute trust in their power. But I know that they are working with me and they respect the trust I place in them.

Do not judge others by what you perceive them to be

At some time in our lives we will project our own negativity onto others – or make snap judgements based on our own perceptions, our prejudices and conditioned responses. Sometimes we judge others through rose-tinted glasses … or bottle-top glasses that equally cloud our vision. Be aware that we live in a hall of mirrors. What is reflected back at us cannot always be trusted. But our minds contain our clarity of vision and it is up to us to nurture that intelligence.

Create the beauty of thoughts, allow them to manifest
all that is wonderful in your life

We should be aware that any destructive thoughts we have are caused by something negative rising within us. It can be centred around our perceived lack of worthiness, the many failings we believe we possess or our preoccupation about how other people view us. We are allowing our egos to take charge and have power over us.

A thought is only a thought. It has no reality beyond the confines of our minds. It is the action that follows the thought that will determine its strength. Our thoughts carry us through each day, firm our decisions, direct us towards our future. Keep your thoughts positive. We should not waste time moaning our way through the mundane tasks we must do. It is easier to enjoy such a task than to resent the fact that it needs to be done. When a problem arises, do not begin the usual cycle of worry, fear and annoyance. Stand back from these emotions and try to observe them calmly. Thinking a problem through rather than responding emotionally will make all the difference to solving it. Have faith that the answer lies within you. That is where your strength of character and insight lies. Believe that your angels are aware of your difficulties and will assist you if you seek their help. A positive thought has the power to achieve great things. A negative thought causes us to stare inwards, naval gazing when we could be reaching for the stars.

Do not hold contempt or un-forgiveness within you,
for they will destroy the essence of who you are

Sorry is often the hardest word to say, yet it is a powerful word. It releases so much tension and resentment within us. Look at how victims of injustice and abuse cry out to their abusers for that one word that will acknowledge their suffering. When we have been wronged it is difficult, sometimes impossible, to forgive. It is up to us to decide whether the weight of our un-forgiveness is mightier than the relief we would feel from letting go of the hurt that haunts us. Trust in the angels to help you make the right decision.

Live your own life
but allow time for others to show you the way

Some people have a wonderful energy around them. I call them 'earthly angels'. They are ordinary people, living heroic lives – carers and healers, and those who radiate a light from within. We meet them and feel an immediate kinship. We are all here on earth to teach each other and, sometimes, the angels open pathways that lead us to like-minded people. These people may have finely tuned psychic abilities or a deep spiritual awareness – and our friendships can be very intense. But Angel Ann tells me that we are only meant to cross each other's paths for a brief while to learn from each other. When that time of learning is over, it is time to move on, as we each continue to travel our individual journeys and open ourselves to new areas of knowledge.

Allow the God of Light into your heart daily for
He is the essence of who you are

I do this through prayer and meditation. But it can be done in many ways. All we have to do is live in the moment and recognise the beauty God has created around us.

You are a twin light within the light of God

God is our Source, our strength, our power. He is the pure reflection of all that is good within us. Look inwards into our hearts for He has many wonderful things to show us. Let us stand tall, knowing that the love of God is guiding and directing our way. Look for the signs and opportunities that He sends us, knowing that they are pathways to help us listen inwardly to His voice. Always believe in the beauty that lives within us.

23

Visualisation and Meditation

Each gift is a learning lesson to strengthen you along the way.
Persevere, even if you become disenchanted and disillusioned.
The life force that guides you also carries you through
those days of loneliness and sadness.

I USED TO RUN MY OWN MEDITATION SESSIONS
when I lived in Blanchardstown. On the first few nights,
people always complained about their restlessness and their
inability to concentrate. But by the end of eight or ten weeks,
it was interesting to see how much they had learned to relax
and be still.

Usually, on the nights that the group came to my house,
Jason and Dwayne would head out with friends to give us
privacy. We had three dogs at the time and I would take them
upstairs until the session finished. On one particular night, we
were settling into a meditative frame of mind when I noticed
that one of the women had a startled expression on her face.

She was staring at the bundle of coats belonging to the group. We had left them piled on one of the chairs near the door. As her expression became more alarmed, I went over to see what was wrong. To my astonishment, I realised that the coats were moving. This movement was an almost wavelike motion, as the coats and jackets rose and settled again. I immediately thought that one of the dogs had escaped from upstairs and burrowed under them. But a quick check confirmed that the three dogs were still upstairs. Our room had grown cold. We were all aware of the change in temperature but no one had any rational explanation as to why the coats were moving. I received no angel messages to explain this strange release of energy. We had been doing a simple meditation and were not trying to communicate with anyone other than our own internal selves. But our combined meditations may have released another energy that manifested itself in our midst. The group was amazed rather than frightened by this demonstration, which eventually died down. We concluded our meditation session, which certainly was the most unusual one we ever held.

Meditation can be a private, solitary act or it can take place within a group. When I first began to meditate, I could only concentrate on a five-minute meditation. The usual domestic thoughts kept intruding. My mind kept straying back to all the chores I needed to finish or the latest family drama that had to be sorted out. I felt almost guilty and self-indulgent for taking this time for myself. I had to learn to set my thoughts free. When these distractions intruded, I allowed them to flow over me and away again by refusing to engage with them. As I persisted, setting aside that short time every day, I was able to stay for longer periods in that stillness. I recognised that the act of meditation was essential if I was to reach a state of mind that would be receptive to the angel messages. But meditation on a more general level helped enormously to bring a sense of harmony and control into my life. My initial five minutes has now extended to an hour a day. Occasionally, especially if I have been working extra-hard and my mind has become too preoccupied, I do a five-minute meditation every hour. I find that this has a powerful effect on my energy. All the irrelevant thoughts disappear and I feel absolutely renewed.

There are some wonderful guided meditation audio CDs that are a great help in the beginning. One that I found particularly useful was *The Beginner's Guide to Meditation* by Joan Z. Borysenko, but it's worth checking out various other publications in spiritual centres or angel shops. If you are finding it difficult to engage in meditation, find a meditation class near you and learn the technique. Once you learn it, you will never forget it. You will also interact with people of similar beliefs. Meditation is a wonderful way to unwind at the end of the day.

Before I begin to meditate, I find a quiet space where I

am unlikely to be disturbed. I light a candle or burn some soothing scented aromatic oils. When the mind seeks stillness, our senses seem to panic and demand to be heeded. So I sit in a comfortable position, making sure I am neither too warm nor too cold, or subject to any outside distractions that can disturb my concentration. I usually begin with a short prayer and put on a CD in the background. This will be soothing or spiritual music with no lyrics, so I won't be distracted by any words.

As I begin to meditate, I become aware of my breathing. It is my life-force energy. When I listen to my breathing, it takes me deeper and deeper into the stillness. Sometimes, in my mind, I take myself on a journey that becomes a visual experience. It depends on my mood. At other times, I engage in a meditation where the focus will be entirely on my breathing. My breath is heavy at first then gradually becomes lighter as I sink deeper into the silence.

I use the following meditation when I am working with a group or leading an angel workshop. This meditation combines a visualisation exercise that focuses on colour and its impact on our senses. It is particularly beneficial if it is done by a facilitator leading a group.

Sit down in a comfortable position.

Allow yourself to relax. Ease the demands of the day from your face. Close your eyes, allow the tension to slide from your mouth, soften you lips. Ease the stress of the day from your shoulders, your arms, your entire body. Let go of all negative thoughts. Banish them from this peaceful space you are creating around yourself. If your thoughts insist on coming to the surface, allow them to do so but don't engage with them. Allow them to float away. They no longer belong to you. They may try to control you, but they cannot harm you.

Take a deep breath. Listen to the sound you make as you draw your breath inwards then release it fully, with your lips slightly open on the exhalation. Repeat this exercise a few times until you feel that you have settled into a rhythmic pattern of breathing.

Repeat the following affirmation to yourself as you inhale. 'I am light.'

As you exhale say, 'I am me.'

Practise this for a few moments, keeping your mind on the words as you breathe in and out. Let your breath draw you into the moment of awareness. Allow the stress of life to have no power over you.

When your mind is totally relaxed and attuned to your meditation, imagine yourself in front of a door. Visualise its colour, the grain in the wood, the door knocker, the latch that you will open. Now, as it swings wide, step inside. Allow yourself to feel that sense of anticipation as your heart reaches out to embrace what you will discover. The room is filled with a powerful red light. It is the red of rose petals, the red of ripened apples, the red sun rising about the red rim of a new day, the red breast of a robin, the flow of red satin. Be as imaginative as you like as you link with this dynamic colour and feel its energy surrounding you. The sky above you is aflame with crimson clouds and your surroundings are bathed in this fiery vigour that uplifts you as it sinks into every part of your being.

When you are ready to leave this room, become aware of another door in front of you. You step inside a room filled with orange colours. Imagine the full harvest moon. An orchard of oranges, hills of gorse, autumn leaves before they fall, pumpkins and peaches, saffron and turmeric. This colour is vivid, spicy, exciting. Orange is a healing colour. Allow its healing energy to ease over you, to penetrate your whole being as you breathe it in. As you do so, become aware of the orange and red colours beginning to merge. As they combine, deepen your breathing and allow them to give you a sense of well-being and vitality.

Soon, when you wish to step from this vibrant colour, become aware of the next door. Walk slowly towards it. You are now about to enter a room filled with sunshine. Its yellow rays are dazzling. You are warmed by the splendour of the sun, charmed by the fields of waving daffodils, the stirring of spring as the forsythia opens and the cowslips blossom. Fill your mind with the cheerfulness of yellow, feel its warmth, its brightness, how it lifts your spirits when the sun shines from a peerless sky. Feel it travel through your veins, encase you heart, ease gently through your mind, which it frees from any negative blocks. Stay with its flowing energy then watch as it gathers the red and the orange into its centre. Then you are ready to move to the next door.

This time the room is filled with another healing colour. Green is grass, green is our island, the sparkle of emeralds, the shade of branches, the shimmer of spring, the scent of meadows. This wonderful colour belongs to nature and to us. We are one. Watch as it grows brighter and brighter and, as it does, imagine a delicate pink light entering the spectrum. Watch as these two shades mingle. Watch them swirling around each other before they merge. Allow yourself to enter them. You are cocooned in love. Unconditional love that demands nothing from you except to sit in serenity and loving peace. This love supports you, heals your emotions, gives you a sense of wonderment, a sense of well-being.

Now it is time for the pink, green, yellow, orange and red colours to form one colour. Allow them to travel over you and work their energies deep into your inner psyche.

It is time to move on. Another door awaits you. Open it and step inside. The sky awaits you. The azure sea surrounds you. Blue is a colour filled with confidence. It is assertive, all-knowing and creative. It cools you down, calms your mind, stills your thoughts. Breathe in the many beautiful shades of forget-me-nots, bluebells, cornflowers and columbines. Do you feel that sense of belief in yourself begin to grow? Grasp it and hold on to it. Trust the emotion. Hear the voice of spirit within you allowing you to push your creativity out into the universe. Relax … breathe … relax … breathe …

Now see the blue, pink, green, yellow, orange and red come together. Each colour has its own power and when they merge, they form a potent force. They are entering you, empowering you, travelling through every part of you. You are suffused in their vitality.

You are now reaching another door. It opens easily. Step inside. This is the purple room and within it there are vast hills of heather, overhanging branches of lilac, clearing filled with shy violets. There are orchards of plum trees and vines heavy with purple grapes. You are surrounded by purple shadows as they fall over the evening sands. Breathe in this colour and, as you do so, watch how it opens up and a triangular shape begins to emerge within it. Watch as this triangular shape slowly begins to move towards you. It is beginning to change shape, growing smaller and smaller. It now begins to resemble an eye. This is your spiritual eye, the eye of clairvoyance, of vision. This eye slowly travels to the centre of your forehead. You can feel its heat as it unites with you and helps you to open up to the clarity you desire. Feel the tingling sensation in your forehead as it begins to penetrate even farther.

Now watch as the purple, blue, pink, green, yellow, orange and red come together. Allow those colours to travel through your body, helping you to raise your vibrations and awareness.

Just relax for a few minutes. You are safe within this wonderful spectrum of colour.

Now, once again, become aware of another door in front of you. Walk towards it, open it and step inside. This room is filled with a wondrous white colour. Breathe deeply. Allow this colour to fill your being. This colour is your bridge between heaven and earth. This is the light of all that is within you. It is your connection to your angels and spirit guides. Rest in its power and know that it can take you to a level of awareness where you can connect to your higher self.

Relax for a few moments in this pure light.

Now it is time to merge these powerful colours. Bring them together – that brilliant white blending with the purple, blue, pink, green, yellow, orange and red.

Watch as they form into your rainbow, into a luminous beam that cradles you, uplifts your spirits, gives you that wonderful sense of vitality and well-being.

Rest in the protection of that rainbow. Your mind is at peace. You are safe and sheltered, embraced in the arms of your angel.

When you are ready to leave this sanctuary, gradually become aware of your body. Slowly, gently, begin to return to the place where you started this journey. Open your eyes, allow them to rest on your surroundings. Shake your hands and wriggle your feet until you feel that every part of your body is once again aligned with you.

This exercise is particularly effective when you feel that you have become disconnected and distracted by too many demands on your time and your emotions. Each of those rooms that you entered had a colour that creates a powerful sense of peace, love and contentment. These colours represent the divinity within you and encourage you to move forward in your life. Allow the time you spend in each room to heal any aspect of your life that is presenting difficulties. Remember you are special. You are part of this universe, powerful in your own standing, and open to the creative flow of colour that lies within you.

I also meditate when I'm out walking. I remain aware of the traffic and my surroundings but I am entering into my spiritual being and not engaging with what's happening around me. I keep repeating this short affirmation:

I walk in the light
I live in the light
I am of the light.

It's a wonderful mind exercise and I come home feeling refreshed and invigorated. All my stresses seem to fall away. I like to think of it as a healing process, especially if my mind is preoccupied with worries.

The gentle rhythm of this affirmation reduces my anxiety level and frees my mind so that it has space to consider and find a solution to my problems. I love walking through parks and forests. As my mind relaxes, my other senses come to the fore. The plants and leaves seem to pulse with energy. The greenery surrounding me has an extra richness and the scents of nature are intoxicating. I don't hear any outside noises, voices, traffic, nothing but birdsong and the rustle of trees.

24

Challenging Situations

We must ask ourselves what is it we really want.
Do we seek the life we richly deserve or do we want
to stay exactly as we are? We have choices. Whatever we choose
for ourselves determines the life we have. We are all one
with the Source who created us. When we feel unworthy,
we separate ourselves from the Source. God has an abundant
flow within Him. It is ours whenever we ask.

SOME PEOPLE BECOME SO DEPENDENT ON THE wisdom of angels that they can't make any decision without consulting them first. This can become a crutch, and I would strongly advise against it. When a decision is life-changing, it is good to seek advice and I have had numerous instances when I have been approached by people who simply want to affirm that they are doing the right thing. However, there are occasions when people refuse to make the simplest choices without first consulting me, or others like me, to affirm every simple decision they have to make. I have learned to discourage such dependency.

At other times, people come to me with an agenda. They only want to hear one message. Anything else is irrelevant. They refuse to take on board the messages they are given and can become very angry, sometimes even aggressive, if that information is not relayed to them. I never feel afraid in such situation. I've done readings in strange places, sometimes in basements when there is only myself and the person who has come for a reading. Thank God I have always been safe, but I am not foolhardy. I have learned caution in my interaction with certain people and to pay attention if my mood changes when an appointment has been made.

Angel Ann has stood back and encouraged me to trust my own intuition and develop my own self-awareness. If I become nervous, restless or uneasy after a certain appointment has been made, I will refuse to take on that reading. I learned this lesson on a fast and steep learning curve. I once booked an angel reading for a woman, whom I'll call Gemma. As soon as I put the phone down, I was conscious of a heavy feeling of dread. This continued for three days and was always triggered when I saw Gemma's name on my appointment list. My instinct was to cancel her reading, but I did not trust my instincts enough to take that decision.

I met Gemma at the arranged time. As soon as I sat down in front of her, I knew I should have heeded the warning signs. It was clear that she was unstable and deeply unhappy. I explained the procedure, but as soon as I asked Angel Ann to give me the correct information, I was answered by silence. No messages, no advice, no reassurances. Nothing. Gemma became increasingly angry when I tried to explain to her that I could not convey any information. She informed me that she went to readings every week and always received messages. I suspected that whoever was doing her readings was taking her money and projecting back at her what she wanted to hear. I could have given her the same reassurance and charged her a fee, which, I suspected, she would have paid willingly. She would have left me in a happy, if deluded, frame of mind. I couldn't do it. Morally, it was reprehensible and it would also have dishonoured the guidance I always received from Angel Ann.

Usually, in emotional situations, the advice that stems from her is abundant. The fact that she had nothing to say had to be significant. I apologised for the lack of information and received a barrage of verbal abuse from Gemma. She was so angry that I was afraid the abuse would turn physical. I was relieved that my son and his friends were in the house and could provide a buffer between us. Eventually she left, having threatened to destroy my reputation.

A similar situation arose when another woman, whom I'll call Carmel, came for a reading. On this occasion, there were no warning vibrations. My chair was in its usual position opposite her, but she insisted on moving her chair and placing it at the end of the room. Angel Ann asked me to ask why she felt this was necessary.

'Because you are in my face,' she replied.

The negative energy that emanated from Carmel washed like a wave over me. That was my warning cue. I should have stopped the reading there and then, but because I wanted to help her, I went ahead. On this occasion, Angel Ann had plenty to say. Carmel was hankering after a love affair that had ended some years previously. She wanted to know if she would be reunited with her ex-partner. When I conveyed this message to Angel Ann, I was told there was no hope of that happening. I was sorry to have to repeat this information, but the truthful answer had to be given, even if it was upsetting. Although Carmel agreed with everything Angel Ann told her about moving on with her life, she refused to accept that the relationship was over. As a result, she sent me abusive texts and made abusive phone calls for days afterwards.

This kind of behaviour was an appalling invasion of my privacy and quite distressing. I learned valuable lessons from both incidents but, thankfully, such experiences are very rare indeed. I realise now that Gemma was so blocked with her own self-absorption that she would not have listened to a word from Angel Ann. She would simply have moved on to the next psychic and the one after that, without making any effort to deal with her own reality. Carmel, on the other hand, knew her relationship was dead, but she had come to me in the hope of receiving a different message. Instead of accepting this truth, which echoed her own, she used her free will to ignore what she had heard. Instead of taking the advice she received from Angel Ann about finding a new direction, she decided to turn her anger on me.

Some people who are sceptical try to trick me by giving false names when they make an appointment. This always puzzles me. By giving me an artificial name, they are destroying my ability to do a true reading. How can I ask for guidance from my angels if the information I relay to them is incorrect? The angels may recognise this deception, but what kind of a relationship does that build between the person who is lying and the spiritual world they wish to contact? During one such reading, I stopped and said to the woman opposite me, 'I've been told by my angel that this is not your real name.'

The woman laughed and agreed that she had been trying to test me. Why? How did she hope that I would be able to work with her when the reading was veiled in trickery? I don't want to hear anyone's life story, but I do need validation. I need to know that I am correctly interpreting the information I receive, especially if I am hearing personal messages from people who have passed on.

When one woman came to me for a reading, I could tell that her husband was seriously ill with a heart condition. Obviously, she was worried about him and deeply concerned about his future. But she was blank-faced and silent as I spoke. She gave an occasional 'maybe' and was obviously unwilling to validate anything I said. Halfway through the reading, I stopped. I was polite but firm when I told her it was over. She seemed startled by my decision and demanded to know why.

'My angel is giving me this information,' I said. 'Is it correct or am I misinterpreting what I am being told? If I'm incorrect, then I am wasting time for both of us. All I want is a yes or no so that it can be validated. Maybe simply does not work for me.'

She said, 'You're perfectly right,' and admitted that she desperately wanted to know that the communication I had with Angel Ann was genuine. She was afraid to trust me in case I was reading her for clues. Obviously, her motives made sense to her, but they interrupted the flow of energy I was receiving. By the end of the session, she was grateful for all the information she had received and left with the belief that she had received a true communication from her angel.

Many people walk away from a reading and say it was fantastic; others are not so impressed with the messages I give them. But all I can do is interpret what I am told and do that to the best of my ability. I cannot embroider or exaggerate the material I receive. I understand why people are sceptical. I have lived with the voices of angels for ten years, but I have never lost the wonder of it or taken it for granted. My dedication to this life must seem strange and suspicious to those who do not believe that there is a higher source of wisdom who communicates with us. But too many things have happened in my life for me to doubt the presence of angels. Many of these incidents are built around my readings. Perhaps that is because I am highly attuned to the needs of the people who come to me, and to the fact that many seek words of comfort from relations who have passed.

Sometimes the signs I receive do not come from the world beyond us. One occasion I will always remember concerned an Asian man who made an appointment for a reading. On the evening before he arrived, I saw an older man, also Asian, sitting in my living room. He sat perfectly still and did not speak. Angel Ann did not relay any message from him nor did I have any clue about why he had materialised. I assumed he was a departed soul and figured he must have been related to the younger man who was due to meet me the following day. I took particular note of the clothes this man was wearing and of his features.

The next day when my client arrived, I could tell from the information I received that his life was in turmoil. These circumstances were outside his control and I felt a deep sympathy for the suffering he was enduring. During the reading, I described the man I had seen the previous day. He immediately recognised his father and he was in no doubt that he had manifested in my living room to bring comfort to his son. But the most surprising aspect of that vision was that his father was still alive and living on the other side of the world.

Something of a similar nature happened when I was living for a short while in rented accommodation in the midlands. A curtain separated the kitchen from the living room, and when I walked towards it one night, intending to switch on the kettle for a cup of tea, I saw a pair of black shoes under the curtain. I stood perfectly still, nervous and undecided whether I should run into the night or investigate this strange phenomenon. Curiosity overcame my fear, and I drew closer. The shoes remained motionless, even though my footsteps could be heard quite clearly. I pulled aside the curtain. There was no one there. Just the shoes. And I knew that they hadn't been there a short while earlier.

The room was suddenly very cold. I heard a voice describing this man's life. It was troubled, filled with conflict, but he was familiar with this house and had spent happy times there. Then the shoes disappeared.

The following day, I asked the owner of the house if any of this information was familiar to him. He was fascinated by the black shoes and immediately recognised the personality I described. When I added that he was a troubled soul, my landlord said, 'Francesca, you have never said a truer word. But he is a troubled soul who is very much alive.'

I don't know why this manifestation took place. I had never spoken to this person then, or since. I cannot interfere in the law of free will and if this troubled person wants the guidance of the angels, it is up to him to seek it.

25
Returning to Ireland

I sit here wondering if everything I did was right.
To leave everything behind and follow the voice of an angel.
To strive for the knowledge she promised me. To leave
my children behind to follow her powerful light.
Was this journey moving me forward so that one day
I could return to Ireland?

LIFE WAS CHANGING FOR FRAN AND ME. AFTER the publication of *My Whispering Angels* many new pathways opened up for me. My angel had told me that the book would bring me back to Ireland, but I had been unable to imagine how that would happen. As more people read the book and word of mouth spread, I began receiving invitations to run workshops and angel evenings in numerous towns and villages around the country. I was amazed by this positive response and thrilled to have the opportunity to visit places I had only ever seen on a map. We now had to divide our time between

Spain and Ireland, and needed to base ourselves somewhere central while we were touring the country. Initially, we stayed for some months in Wexford, then moved to Bruff in County Limerick.

This was not a random decision. I was guided there by my friend Joanne, whom I had met two years previously when she participated in an angel workshop I conducted in Limerick. Joanne has a beautiful character and I warmed to her immediately. She too believed in angels and I could see that she had a wonderful connection to them. When we finished the workshop we decided to stay in touch and quickly became friends. Joanne introduced me and Fran to her family, her husband Don and their three sons. We also met her extended family, who are as friendly and warm as Joanne.

At that time, Fran and I were trying to set up a website. This was proving to be more difficult than we had anticipated and finding the right person to advise us was proving to be a nightmare. My belief that the angels guide us to each other was proved once again when Fran mentioned the technical problems we were having to Joanne. She smiled and said she knew the exact person who could help us. Her husband Don works with computers. As soon as we explained our problems to Don, he came up with great ideas that helped us to design the exact website we wanted.

Through our contact with this lovely couple, we found a small cottage in the country and based ourselves there.

Everything in this cottage was old and full of character. I soon realised that it was also full of spirits. But they did not frighten or disturb us. They were the spirits of the people who were connected to the area, a place that still held comfort and love for them. As I sat in silence with my angels, I know I was very much at one with them. I have often wondered why we find ourselves in certain places at certain times in our lives. Are we led there for a reason? My time in Bruff proved that this is true in many ways.

I had never lived in a rural environment. Our life in Dublin had been suburban and our home in Spain is surrounded by other houses. In Bruff, I had to become accustomed to solitude and silence. I had to forget the faster, more familiar pace of life and slow down to a different rhythm. I loved meditating in the garden where the birdsong and the droning of bees provided peaceful background music. I discovered the beauty of the countryside, in particular the tranquillity of Lough Gur, famous for its archaeological sites. I loved to explore the area, knowing that the remains of so many periods of Irish history – from the Stone Age through to post-medieval times – have been preserved. It became another favourite place to meditate and visualise, and I always came back feeling refreshed and revived.

Anyone who needs to sit in silence and be at ease with their angels should go there and experience its peace. The lake has its own store of folklore and one story that particularly interested me was that of Gearoid Iarla Fitzgerald, the third Earl of Desmond and Chief Justice of Ireland in 1367, following the Statutes of Kilkenny. It is claimed that his conception was magical and that, not surprisingly, he practised magic spells throughout his life. These included turning himself into a goose and a goldfinch.

According to local folklore, as a punishment for his involvement in magic, he did not die but lives beneath the waters of the lake. As I sat on the shore and stared into the tranquil waters, I wondered about his magic and how such folk legends had originated. Had he been gifted with finely tuned psychic abilities? Had he the power to mesmerise those around him? I was hoping I might sense his presence. He never appeared, although he is reputed to ride around the lakeshore on his white horse once every seven years. His horse is shod with silver shoes and when the shoes are finally worn down, he will return in his human form and restore the glory of the Desmonds.

Although I saw no sign of the earl or his horse, I did awaken one night in my cottage to see a young woman standing in the bedroom. I knew I was not dreaming. The room was cold and, although the woman was surrounded by a dull yellow glow, I could see her clearly. She carried a baby in her arms. Her clothes belonged to a bygone era and were well worn. She told me her name was Kathleen Roe. She had been murdered but her baby had died two days before her own tragic death. She said the wrong man had been accused of the crime. That was all the information I received before she faded away. I woke Fran and told him what had happened. He had experienced enough of my manifestations to believe me, but I was only able to relay this scant information to him. I made enquiries in the local area to see if I could find out anything about this young woman's history. No one could tell me anything about her. She belonged to an age long past and the truth of her tragic story still remains untold.

The Grange circle was another place that drew me into its centre. It is the largest stone circle in Ireland and was built during the Bronze Age. I visited it with Fran when we first arrived in Bruff. My mood was quite despondent that day and, as everything in my life was going quite well, I wanted to understand this feeling. As I walked around the circle, I felt my spirits tune into the peaceful atmosphere. I sat on one of the rocks and it seemed as if a cleansing of my negative energy was beginning to take place. I was conscious of being in the moment and I could feel my angels gathering around me. Instinctively, I knew they had brought me here for a reason.

I noticed that Fran was talking to a man who had been standing in the stone circle when we arrived. I left them alone and remained sitting on the rock. The energy continued to build around and within me. I allowed it to flow through my body and waited to see what would happen. I noticed the man walking towards me. We acknowledged each other with a simple hello. Something about him bothered me. I reached out to shake his hand. As our hands touched, I realised he was in need of healing. I could almost feel his pain and I understood that the angels had guided us both to this ancient place for a reason. I asked him if he believed in angels. When he smiled and nodded, I knew that he had a deep connection to them.

I explained to him about my own association with the angels and that I had been communicating with them for many years. I explained the sensation that had swept through me when I shook his hand. He sighed, as if he understood. I then asked if I could relay a message I had received about him from Angel Ann. He was more than happy to listen. I began to explain about the deep issues he had within him, especially around his father. The anger, the hurt he still carried over from his boyhood.

I am always astonished by the many young and not-so-young men who carry deep-seated, negative feelings within them about their fathers. It can be a complex relationship, especially when so many fathers of previous generations had little to do with their children's upbringing. In those harsher times, one of their main paternal roles was to administer punishment when children misbehaved. The emotional blocks this created between sons and fathers are often carried into the next generation and so it can manifest itself when I am doing a reading.

This man needed to heal and let go if he was to find the

peace he needed. We spoke for some time. He understood everything that the angels had to say to him. He was on holiday in Ireland. Just before he came to the stone circle, he had visited Glenstal Abbey, which is not far from where we met. He was feeling particularly low at that time and had gone into the church to speak to God. He had been searching for answers to his life, to his direction, his purpose. He had asked God to send him a sign that he was being heard. As he sat there, he heard a voice telling him to go to the stone circle in Grange. He would find his answer there. He was unsure how this voice had reached him, as he was alone in the church. But he did as he was asked and made his way to the stone circle.

This man – with all his hurt and unresolved memories – was beginning a journey to become a healer. He had been aware of his healing abilities for a long time but was not sure which way to go. Now God was guiding him and he understood the significance of our meeting. I assured him that the path he was choosing was the right one. When he thanked me and walked away I knew that he was going to be okay. I stood for a while longer within the centre of this ancient and historical stone circle and thanked my angels. They had guided me there to affirm this man's decision and, in doing so, I had also helped myself. My negative energy had gone. A healing had taken place within me and as I left this place of stone it felt wonderful to be alive.

Mother and daughter relationships can also have their

difficulties. On one occasion, two women, Diana and Sharon, booked to see me together but, as they had different surnames, I didn't make any connection between them. Diana rearranged her reading for two days later, but I went ahead with Sharon's reading as planned. She was young and married, and had some serious problems with her husband.

During the reading I said to her, 'Why isn't your mother listening to you instead of taking your husband's side?'

The relief on Sharon's face was touching. It seemed as if someone had reached out to understand her hurt for the first time. She admitted that her mother refused to listen to her side of the story. She believed Sharon should be grateful that she was married to this man and seemed incapable of appreciating any other point of view. But Sharon desperately needed her mother to be her anchor. The fact that this support was not forthcoming was causing her extreme distress. She was my last reading for that day and she left with a taped recording of her angel messages.

Two days later, Diana came to see me. When I was about to communicate with her I spoke internally to Angel Ann, as I always do, and said, 'Help me to do this work.'

I felt an energy charge. It built into a tremendous force and was accompanied by a strong white light. I knew that this energy came from the spirit world and that it was a female presence. Angel Ann was by my side, speaking into my right ear, as she always does. Her voice was as clear as a bell when she told me that this spirit was Diana's mother. The first message she gave Diana was, 'Please take care of your daughter. She is extremely unhappy and needs your support.'

From then on, the focus of the reading was about Diana's relationship with her daughter. When the reading ended, I was surprised to discover that the daughter in question was Sharon. She had left the recording I had made of her reading with Diana, who had had time to listen to it before she came to me for her own reading. As a result, she had arrived with an open mind and when her own mother came from the spirit world to speak to her, she was able to listen and understand the message. The readings proved to be a great source of healing for both Sharon and Diana – and their relationship has become stronger and more supportive since that day.

26

An Ocean of Plenty

*You have the ability to seek the many qualities within you.
Use them wisely and they will bring many positive changes
into your life. Do not doubt yourself. You are confident.
You are strong. Acknowledge yourself. You are a beautiful
human being with the capabilities to change whatever
it is that makes you unhappy.*

WE DO NOT NEED THE ANGELS TO TELL US THAT
obesity has become a serious health issue. The foods we eat have
a determining effect on our weight and well-being. We can
always improve our health by being aware of our thoughts and
actions. But being aware of what is good for us is not enough.
We must have the self-discipline to put that knowledge into
practice.

Why do we choose to do certain things when we know they
have a negative impact on us? Why do we keep making excuses
when we behave in a way that is detrimental to our physical

and emotional health? Often the foods we enjoy are the fast and processed foods that do the most damage to our bodies. If we want to feel stronger, more energetic and healthier, we must eliminate these toxins from our system and establish a balanced way of living.

Birds love berries, but avoid the poisonous ones. They are tuned to the demands of their bodies and we too can reach the same level of awareness by inwardly fine-tuning our consciousness. Meditate on our bodies to see how we can improve our well-being. Initially, this may seem like a strange form of meditation but it will focus our determination. Every time you reach for something to eat that you know is not good for you, ask your body how it feels about consuming it. If you listen, you will always receive an answer.

We should exercise for a short while every day. Start small and build up your endurance. Join a gym or keep fit class if it helps you to be more disciplined. Remember that walking is one of the healthiest exercises you can undertake and, as I mentioned in a previous chapter, you can also use it as a form of meditation. As your health improves so will your mood. You will be uplifted in mind, body and spirit. This sense of wellness will encourage you to keep up the good habits you have established. It takes time to train your thoughts in a positive way and be consistent.

Begin by establishing realistic goals, especially when it comes to the area of weight loss. Release all the bad habits you have acquired over the years. Let them go in a gentle and positive way. As always, you have free will and the choices you make will determine the outcome.

Sometimes the weight we carry is not physical. When life becomes too serious and demanding, it weighs us down. Over time, you become so accustomed to carrying this weight that you are no longer conscious of the heaviness in your shoulders.

Society labels us into different classes. We are streamed into the 'haves' and the 'have nots'. Some people are born into an environment where opportunities are taken for granted. They will receive a better education, have easier access to university, followed by a professional career, often within a closed and protective profession. On the other side, we have large disadvantaged areas, a poor health system, a breakdown in the family unit and many more associated problems. Governments make promises but change is slow and littered with broken pledges. What this reveals is that society is telling us that some of us are worthy and others are unworthy.

But only we can make this assessment. It is our perception of ourselves that counts. If we each believed that we have the ability through the power of our thinking to create the life we want, then we would have a society of equals. Are we not all embodied with the Source that created us? Yes, we are. When we feel unworthy, we are separating ourselves from this Source.

We must ask ourselves if we want the life we richly deserve

or if we want to stay exactly as we are. We all have choices. Whatever we choose determines our future. God has an abundant flow within Him and it is ours when we seek it.

We must learn to live in the here and now. We must not forget to enjoy the simple things in life, a walk in sunshine, time spent with friends, taking time out to watch a funny film, telling someone you love them – without expecting anything in return. Laughter is a wonderful source of health. It nourishes our souls and promotes a strong sense of well-being and contentment within us.

Our mind wants to control our thoughts and our actions. When we begin to merge within our spirit, we come to an awareness that we are much more than what we see. Our existence is based on our conscious awareness that we are a light within a light. We must be aware of our negative thoughts when they arise. Do not fear them. Heal them. Let them go. When we come to understand and experience this freedom, the stress of daily life cannot touch us.

What can we do to improve things? We have the power to deal in a peaceful way with any stressful situation that comes along. That power is our God power, our Source. Every time you find yourself in a negative situation, affirm:

I am a child of God, nothing can touch me.

I am a child of God, nothing can touch me.

I am a child of God, nothing can touch me.

Let us imagine a great ocean in front of us. It is filled with all we desire in life. If we could gather in the rich harvest it provides, would we? Or would we turn our backs on all it offers? If we choose the latter, why do we do so? Are we afraid to change the negative pattern in our lives? Is our self-esteem so low that we do not feel we deserve the best? Do we feel safer walking through the debris that we have piled up around us? Is it easier to accept this familiar wasteland of lost hopes and dreams than to dare believe there is another way?

Do we understand the reasons why we continue to have certain problems in our lives? Are we aware of why we carry out certain actions? When we understand the reasons for our behavioural pattern, we are able to recognise the issues that are influencing us. Only then will we learn to take control of our lives in ways that will lead us to a desired outcome.

Look towards the ocean and turn your back on the wasteland. It is an arid, lonely place and we were never meant to occupy it. Look for the alternative. It is rich beyond our wildest dreams, not in material possessions but in the joy we will possess when we release ourselves from everything that holds us back. Allow the ocean to carry us forward and provide us with the self-belief to make that move with absolute confidence.

Ocean	Wasteland
People	Lack
Places	No confidence

Opportunities	Low self-esteem
Career	Not worthy
Joy, happiness	Nothing good ever happens
Fulfilment	No desire to fulfil in life
Prosperity, abundance	Always poor, always complaining
I believe in me and in what I do	Always sick and yet nothing physically wrong
I love me, I am beautiful	Blame others for things going wrong in my life
I am a wonderful, intelligent human being	I am horrible, life is unfair
I have a great ability within me to create opportunities in my life	I am ugly, who would want me?
I create only good in my life	If I lose that extra weight then I will be happy
I am healthy	If I had the right relationship …
My relationship with my family and friends is beautiful	Good things are meant for other people, but not for me.
I have a healthy and loving relationship with my children	Nobody cares
I allow myself the freedom to choose	
My life flows in a positive way	

27

Journeying Onwards

As we walk hand in hand with our spirit, we will always
find a connection to the many things around us. We will
be guided into unknown territories. We worry if we will
be accepted into each new stage, not realising that the world
of spirit has already set a place for us, to learn, to seek,
to teach that our life is an amazing journey.

IN THE EARLY YEARS, AS MY MIND STRUGGLED TO
accept the new reality that had entered my life, I often wondered
if I was dreaming. But the distinction between dreams and my
visionary encounters was as separate as night and day. I slept and
dreamed, woke and entered the realm of angels. But there was a
twilight dimension that, on a few occasions, bridged those two
worlds.

In one particularly vivid dream, I found myself in Los
Angeles, a place I had never visited. I was walking along a
beach, accompanied by a woman. She was a stranger, yet we

walked together in a companionable silence, at ease in each other's company. I woke the next morning with complete recall of the dream and, instead of it fading, as dreams usually do, this one remained with me in all its details throughout the day. That night the dream returned and each detail was exactly the same. The same sandy shore, the sun shining on my shoulders, the quiet, serene woman walking step-by-step with me.

At a certain point on the beach she stopped and smiled at me. 'I have to leave now,' she said. 'But you keep walking on.'

I asked her name. She told me it was Betty. 'I'm from the Inner Light Foundation,' she said and, with those words ringing in my head, I woke. The Inner Light Foundation. I wondered if I had read the words somewhere or seen them on an advertisement. I looked through my books but could not see any mention of it anywhere. I rang my sister, Elaine.

Elaine is an insightful interpreter of dreams. Usually, when a dream puzzles me and I feel it has a particular significance, I ring her for an interpretation. I may not always like the information she gives me. Sometimes it stops me in my tracks and forces me to change my opinion because I know she is wise and always right.

On this occasion, she was as puzzled as I was. She had never heard of the Inner Light Foundation, but she suggested I check the internet and see if it existed. To my surprise, I came across a foundation of that name in Los Angeles. I emailed them and described my dream in detail. I included the words that

Betty had exchanged with me. A man emailed back. He was involved with the Inner Light Foundation and he was able to tell me that the woman who had founded it was Betty Bethards, widely known as a spiritual healer, psychic and mystic. She was also affectionately known as the 'Common Sense Guru'.

She had died in 2002, some months before I had dream-walked with her on that beach. The more I discovered about her, the more I was intrigued by the life she had led. She had helped many people understand the cycles and stages of life, including their final journey into the spirit world. She had had a near-death experience in her thirties and this had left her with a fearless attitude to death.

'After my first death experience, I lost all fear of dying,' she said. 'I realised that life and death are part of a continuum of being. Then I began to find real meaning of my life here on earth. Death is nothing more than leaving the body, just like we do every night in the dream state. We all leave the body at night. If you jerk as you are falling asleep, it's a bad take-off. If you dream you are falling, it's a bad landing coming in. If you waken but can't move your body, you haven't fully merged with it yet. Just take a few deep breaths, relax and you'll be fine.'

I'd love to have met her in real life, but that was not to be. However, I have always remembered the serenity of her presence as we walked together along that beach. I'd like to think she came to encourage me to trust the wisdom of my angels but to remain grounded to the reality of my own life. In other words, to never lose my common-sense approach as I opened myself to new revelations.

Perhaps this sense of leaving my body is the reason I've become increasingly interested in shamanism. This ancient spiritual and healing tradition has been practised for over 50,000 years and is an extension of the love I feel for nature and my connection to Mother Earth. I love the idea of drumming, which is an essential feature of shamanic ritual. The rapid beat is known to change the brainwaves to a deeper level of awareness and I was interested in discovering more about it.

I knew that within the traditions of shamanism, there is a recognition of three worlds.

In the Lower World, we make contact with all of nature, its creatures and plants, and our power animals. This primeval knowledge can help us heal each other and heal the earth that is being torn apart and abused by so many for so little gain.

Middle World is the world we inhabit, our past, present and future. This is where we discover our mission and find the means to draw on the wisdom of our ancestors.

The Upper World is where we make contact with our spirit guides and angels, and seek communion with those souls who have passed to the other side. This is where we search for the bigger messages in our daily interaction with our angels.

I made enquiries in Spain to learn more about shamanism, but could find no suitable courses on offer. When I mentioned this desire to Angel Ann, she told me that I would find an envelope with the information I needed in my post box the following day. To my surprise, when I opened my post the next morning, I discovered a brochure from Shamanism Ireland, advertising a weekend workshop at its venue, Dunderry Park in County Meath, which is close to the ancient sacred sites of Tara, Newgrange and Loughcrew. I'd completely forgotten that I'd put my name down for a shamanic weekend when I attended a Mind Body Spirit show in the RDS in Dublin earlier that year. This course was centred on communing with nature and the natural elements and was not the one I had originally picked out. My chosen one was booked up and this was being offered as an alternative.

I rang and booked into the course. I discovered that the only food on offer for the weekend would be vegetarian. My heard sank. I imagined dull stir-fries and bland rice dishes. I have never been a fan of vegetarian food, and my eyes always skimmed over the vegetarian options on the menu when I was in a restaurant. I pushed back my disappointment and agreed to go with the flow.

Elaine arranged to collect me at Dublin airport. The course was beginning at seven that evening and the traffic, when we left the airport, was bumper to bumper. We travelled at a snail's pace, and I became increasingly aware that there was no way I would make the opening lectures. Elaine was driving her husband's taxi and as we stopped, yet again, at another set of traffic lights, I heard a voice inside my head demanding to know if Elaine or myself had a brain cell between us. I recognised that voice. Angel Ann was back on duty. I asked her what exactly she meant and she said, 'What is on the top of this car?'

'A taxi sign,' I said.

'And what is to the side of you?' she asked.

'A taxi lane.'

I related this to Elaine, who said, 'I can't possibly switch on that taxi sign. It's too risky.' We were more than ever convinced that this was the case when we noticed a police car on the other side of us. When I reported this back to Angel Ann she advised me that there was enough light around this car for the sign to be switched on without anyone noticing.

'Go for it,' I said to Elaine. 'We have been divinely instructed to use the taxi lane.' And that is exactly what we did. We reached Dunderry Park in thirty minutes flat and in perfect time to begin one of the most amazing weekends I ever experienced. As for Angel Ann and her disregard for traffic regulations, she warned me that that was a one-off violation, never to be repeated.

From the moment I entered Dunderry Park, I knew I was going to enjoy myself. Everything was explained to us in a very simple way.

On Saturday, we were asked to go outside and connect with nature. We had to see if we were drawn to a particular tree.

The angels tell us that there is energy in nature and that was what I experienced. I allowed my mind to free itself from any inhibitions and walked where the energy led me to one of the beautiful old trees in the grounds of this magnificent Georgian estate.

In the afternoon, we repeated the exercise, only this time we were asked to see if we were drawn in the direction of a certain plant. I approached a plant and as I bent towards it, I noticed that it was moving. The wind was not blowing and everything around me was still, apart from this plant, which swirled and twirled, as if it was dancing to an inaudible melody. My senses were so attuned to what was taking place before my eyes that I was not surprised when I heard a little voice encouraging me to bend down and pick the plant.

It was amazing to feel so linked to the earth. A new path of learning had been opened up for me and I realised that I still had so much more to learn about the forces of nature and my relationship to them. As for the vegetarian meals, I completely changed my attitude and enjoyed some of the most wonderful meals I have ever tasted.

28

An Interview with Francesca

What is this road the angels take us on? What lies so deep within us that they need us to discover? Is it that we have lost our way? Lost our identities? To truly understand the concept of our lives, must we go back before we can go forwards? Someone once said that the world of angels and spirit guides was beautiful but also difficult. I have come to believe in those words. They have been a significant part in my journey.

I AM SOMETIMES QUESTIONED BY PEOPLE WHO are cynical about the work I do. I always respond to such questions as honestly as I can – but I never pretend to have all the answers. My angel experience is personal to me. I am an angel messenger and the gifts they have given me help me fulfil that role. I leave the theorising and speculating to others, like my sister Elaine, for instance, whose knowledge of the existence of the angel realm and its purpose is profound. My function is to pass on their wisdom and guidance to those who seek it. The following is a compilation of the questions I am most often asked.

Question: I don't see angels. Therefore they can't exist.

Francesca: Can you see the air you breathe? Can you see gravity, space, your inner voice, your energy, the wind that separates a leaf from a tree, the petals from a flower? Can you see the power that silences our final breath? We have radio waves and telephone masts beaming signals at each other. We experience but we don't see the sounds we make, no matter how beautiful they are, nor can we see that wonderful scent of cut grass or bread baking. Our world is filled with invisibility, which we accept without question, because we know these immaterial things exist within its sphere.

My angels came to me and I accepted their presence. You can accept their existence or reject it. Each of us possesses the law of free will. Angels tell me I am not here to prove their existence. I am here to do their work.

Question: Will I ever see an angel if I don't believe in their existence?

Francesca: If your mind is closed to their existence, then probably not. This is where faith comes to the fore. Sometimes, when people are in an extreme life-threatening situation, an angel will suddenly manifest her presence. It could be just a flash, an instant of awareness that, afterwards, could easily be rejected as imagination. But there have been too many such manifestations, especially to non-believers, to dismiss them so easily.

One woman told me how, when she was driving one day, she heard a voice warning her to fasten her seatbelt. The voice was so insistent that she stopped the car and belted up. About a minute later she rounded a bend and her car skidded. When she pulled on the steering wheel, her car went out of control and hit an embankment. It turned upside down before righting itself again. She was uninjured because she was strapped in. She was a non-believer but I believe she heard the voice of her guardian angel.

I also spoke to a young Asian woman who had lost a number of her relations, including her mother, during the terrible tsunami that claimed so many lives in 2004. Some years before, when her house was being built, she had heard an inner voice instructing her to insist on concrete foundations. Concrete was not a traditional method used for constructing houses in her country, but the builder did as she requested. She survived the tsunami and her house remained standing while those around her were destroyed. She believed she had been guided by her angel and had been open to that inner voice. But angels will not appear to us simply to prove their existence.

Question: How did angels originate?

Francesca: Angels were always a source of light and did not originate on this earth. They are beings of pure light and energy. They exist to guide and guard us through our lives.

We depict them with wings and human characteristics, but that is purely an aid to help us identify them. My first angel manifestation was a stream of light and, because I was confused, Angel Ann appeared the next time as a figure I could identify. As my confidence grew and my trust in her became absolute, she no longer needed to appear in that shape. I recognise her light as soon as she appears. It is only when I'm faced with difficulties that she now appears in that familiar form to comfort me.

Question: Is God the source of light?

Francesca: Yes. As a Christian, I believe that God is an all-powerful source of light, compassion and wisdom. He is served by His angels who intercede on our behalf.

Question: Where do angels reside?

Francesca: They are within us, around us, everywhere.

Question: What do you mean when you say our angels are within us? I thought they were separate entities?

Francesca: Why must there be a separation? We are spiritual beings united within our physical presence. We cannot separate our daily lives from our spiritual existence. If we choose, we can open up to the angel power within us and use it in a creative and constructive way.

Question: Can this angel power be our imagination at its most powerful?

Francesca: No. They are two separate energies. The angel influence is an energy you won't experience under any other circumstances, even when your imagination is fuelled with desire or adrenaline. The accuracy of the messages I receive, and the visions that accompany them, are gifted to me by a divine ordinance and I have learned to trust this sublime power.

The first step is to recognise that we have that God-force energy – but it is only in the stillness of meditation that we can reach that place. It has taken years of dedicated and profound meditation for me to achieve that level of awareness. In the early stages, my mind kept getting in the way, demanding to know why my wishes and prayers were not answered immediately. My negative thoughts would then take over and I would flounder, striving all the time to understand the mystery of the source.

The angels tell us to take our thoughts inwards. As we empty our minds, our soul takes over. Even today, my thoughts will interfere but I allow them to journey on. I do not allow them to trouble me, nor do I engage with them. They are fleeting fragments with no power over me. Sometimes I say to my angels, 'What do you need me to know?'

This time last year I asked them what they wanted, and they said, 'No limitation around your work.'

Question: So you accept the angels on trust?

Francesca: Yes. When I welcomed them into my life I surrendered myself to them. Put at its simplest, that means that I believe in their existence. At its most complex, it means that I relinquished my old life. I cast off all the conditionings and ways of thinking that had influenced me in the past and I now follow their guidance. I believe utterly in the higher power of the Divine Source to guide my life.

Question: Does everyone have their own angel?

Francesca: Yes. Their ordained task is to walk with us and protect us. But many of us will go through life without any awareness that they are our guardians. If we learn to listen to their voices as they echo within us, we will become aware of their power. I've spoken to many people from other religions and they all share a common awareness of angels and how they can effect change in their lives.

Question: Is an angel the same as a spirit guide?

Francesca: No. A spirit guide is the evolved spirit of someone who has passed from this earth. They are special people who once lived their lives to its fullest potential. Their purpose is to encourage us to do the same. On occasions, I work with spirit guides, in particular with a black American called Eamon, who has a terrific sense of humour. Spirit guides bring great comfort to those of us living on earth, but an angel will bring us closer to God.

In the early stages of my journey with my angels, I enrolled on a course that studied the human aura. As we meditated I saw a Native American Indian appear behind the woman who was running the course. By the time the class ended, I had witnessed this image for a second time. On this occasion, the man was accompanied by a woman, dressed in the same type of clothing. An animal that I took to be a wolf stood beside them. I discovered at the end of the class that the course leader was descended from Native American Indians. When I told her about the apparitions, including the wolf, she smiled and told me that he was her grandfather's dog. The two people I described were her grandparents who had raised her on an Indian reservation in Alaska. They looked upon her with such affection and pride that I have to assume they are her spirit guides.

Question: Is it necessary to have a life-changing trauma to experience the presence of angels?

Francesca: No, although there are many people who are guided to this work when their lives are in trauma. But, nowadays, I'm constantly astonished by the number of young people who are willing to place their trust in angels. They have an openness and spiritual awareness that is wonderful to behold. I encounter them in my workshops and my angel evenings and I can tell immediately that they will spread the positive vibrations of angels wherever they go.

Sadly, against this positivity there are many young people opting out of lives through drugs or suicide. When they come to me for readings, I see a dark density around them. Their minds are so blocked that nothing I, or anyone else, says will get through to them. They themselves must reach into their own souls and decide to take the path to recovery.

When we learn to live from the inside, we have this ability to effect change. We are born with everything we need to help us live to our full potential. But many other outside factors get in the way. From the moment of birth, we are conditioned by our culture, our family values, our surroundings, our traditions and our beliefs. We accept this as natural. We are part of the greater society. But do we ever stop to wonder where we – the individual I – are in this great morass? Have we formed our own set of beliefs? Questioned the perceived values that were handed to us? Accepted, without question, that we have a clearly defined role to follow within this society or family unit? Are we aware of a lack in our lives, a vague disquiet that we are missing something essential, despite the fact that we have everything we need for happiness? Or, if we are coping with great difficulties, are we stranded on that island of unhappiness, unable to move forwards because of conditioning, fear or the great loss of self?

These are big questions with no easy answers – but I was forced to consider them when I became aware that I could hear the voices of angels calling out a different message to me.

Question: You talk about shifts in consciousness; can you be more specific?

Francesca: More and more in my work, I come across people who are being led down pathways of wisdom and opening up to a whole new way of thinking. They want to know if there is more to themselves than what they see and experience. They want to look beyond the conditioning of Church, state and family, and seek their own awareness. When I listen to them, it is like hearing my own voice echoing back at me – and I know they are awakening to their inner spirituality. Sometimes we are forced to pause in life and reflect on where we are going. This pause can occur when someone we love dies and their loss compels us to consider what happens after death. Does life continue in another form or is that the end of everything? I believe it is only the beginning. For me, ME was my spiritual awakening. I've been surprised by the number of people who have been affected by this disease and who came into an awareness of spirit as they regained their strength.

Question: What prevents us tuning into our angels?

Francesca: Our minds get in the way. We demand hard facts, evidence. Like the apostle Thomas, we want to place our hands in the wounds and feel the holes. There is also fear. To follow my path, I had to trust. But it can take years to reach that level of trust. Trust leaves us vulnerable. Trust takes away our control. Trust demands a letting go of all that is familiar in our thought process.

Question: Can you ignore the angels when they call?

Francesca: Yes. We can exercise our own free will. I knew a man who had a deep need within him to follow a spiritual pathway. His family were totally opposed to the idea. For twenty years, he listened to their voices and worked in a day job that crushed any joy of life from him. But he was earning a good living and supporting his family. To move from that circle of security and enter a wilderness of uncertainty seemed impossible. He managed to keep his unhappiness under control until he attended a lecture about fear and how it controls us. He was so moved by this lecture that he decided to make a change in his life and follow his inclinations. This was the shift within him and it was enormous. He walked away from his secure job and the day he walked out the door of that office, the weight that he had carried for so long on his shoulders lightened. He had stopped noticing the burden he carried until it disappeared. Since then, he has followed his own spiritual inclination and he has never looked back.

Question: What do your angels expect from you?

Francesca: They don't expect anything. All I have to do is the best I can. If I wanted to give this work up tomorrow, I could do so and there would be no pressure. Free will is mine.

Question: Do you let the angels to make all your decisions for you?

Francesca: When I ask for their help they give it to me and I listen for that inner voice. But they also stand back and allow me to make my own decisions. They are still there supporting me but they encourage me to think independently, to believe in my own ability to make the right choices. When something feels right, I go for it. If I am undecided, I turn to them for guidance.

Question: Are you in a hurry to increase your pathways of learning?

Francesca: Yes, I am. Sometimes I am in too much of a hurry. I yearn to go further inwards into my spiritual awareness. But I must go at the pace that Angel Ann outlines to me. I've had to learn to have patience.

If I was looking for a simple comparison, I would describe this learning experience to a term in angel school. I learn one lesson and then I move on to the next grade. When I reach that next grade, I feel a sense of restlessness. I want to reach out towards my next encounter. Looking back on my journey, which started ten years ago, I can see the vast distance I have travelled. When I look to the future, it is luminous with promise. But the one lesson I have learned from the angels, is that I must live in the moment. The 'now' is what matters. When they are ready to bring me forwards, I will be prepared.

When I held my first angel evening, I was terrified as the date drew nearer. Only for the calm voice of Angel Ann assuring me that I would be okay, I would have cancelled the event. I had expected a small crowd to attend and was shocked as the room began to fill with people of all ages. I began the evening with an introductory talk and angel meditation. After I had finished, I felt a surge of absolute panic. 'What do I do now?' I asked Angel Ann.

'Align your vibrations with me and trust me,' she said. 'See that white-haired man in the third row? Let the light guide you to him.'

And that was exactly what happened. I relaxed and communicated with his loved one and the energy gathered strength in the room.

When it was over I said to the angel, 'You threw me in at the deep end. Why didn't you warn me that there would be such a large crowd?'

'I threw you in at the deep end because you were ready,' she replied. 'If I had told you what to expect, your mind would have interfered and your nervousness would have taken over. Now you know you have moved on to the next level and you are ready to move forwards.'

Question: Can you explain angel vibrations?

Francesca: It's an intense tingling sensation that brings a surge of energy with it. Sometimes I feel it coming through my shoulder blades and travelling along my spine. The energy of our angels is many times stronger than our own. Their vibrations are pure and subtle but our vibrations are probably much more dense. In order for them to communicate with us, they have to bring their vibrations down to our level and we have to be in a calm, meditative state to receive them.

Question: Will our angel come to us at our hour of death?

Francesca: Everyone is guided home by their angel. Sometimes our loved ones come to us and we often hear of people's expressions becoming suffused with warmth and welcome as they are drawing their final breath. I can only assume that they are being welcomed home.

Question: Have you a memory of previous lives you lived on this earth?

Francesca: This is not a question I can answer with complete confidence. When this heavenly light appeared to me as I sat by the pool in Spain and said, 'I am,' I believed I was in the presence of Jesus, son of God – but I cannot be sure. He is an embedded memory that I have not yet brought to the surface. All I have is an awareness that I once walked this earth with Him and listened to His voice. Perhaps the answer awaits me as I go deeper into a meditative state. When this awareness happens, I will know that I have reached another stage of my journey.

Question: When you say that all that we need is 'within us', what do mean?

Francesca: Angels come from the deepest part of us, which is our soul. Their light and energy comes from God and they tell us that we are not separated from Him. He is within each one of us and the more we learn to connect with the Source, the more we understand that we are one with that power.

Question: Are there bad angels – as in negative and positive vibrations?

Francesca: My angels have never revealed the existence of bad angels. I've always only had the most positive encounters with my spirit guides and angels. I don't believe in Lucifer. My personal belief is that he was created by man and the religious organisations that build a fear of creed around him. We only have to look at the magnificent but horrifyingly graphic images in the paintings of artists down through the centuries to see how influential Lucifer was.

I've read angel books and spoken to angel communicators who claim to have encountered evil spirits. I once sat in a healer's room and felt a deep calm settling over me. The atmosphere was meditative and I could almost touch the feeling of being in a good and wholesome place. When I commented on this, the healer agreed that there were many good angels present and their main purpose was to stop the evil spirits from entering. She was convinced they would invade her space if her angelic forces released their guard. I felt none of the conflict between good and bad that she described. I could only wonder if this conflict was due to her physical rather than her spiritual issues. In truth, I have never encountered an evil entity and don't believe I ever will.

Even with exorcism, I have my own views and wonder if

such manifestations are brought about by extreme mental conflicts. Each person travels their own journey and my angels are a source of light. They do not cast shades of darkness.

Question: Do dogs cross over to the spirit world?

Francesca: People who don't have pets or have no affinity with animals find it very difficult to understand the grief we feel when a family pet dies. But losing a pet can be a traumatic experience, especially when it has been part of our family for many years. We've always had dogs, each with his or her own quirky personality. For people living on their own, their pet can be their best friend and they are distraught when this companion dies.

Recently, I was contacted by the presenter of a radio programme and asked if dogs passed on to another dimension when they die. According to Angel Ann, they do.

When I started out on this journey ten years ago, we had three bichons – Holly, Kissy and Cassy. Holly was the first to leave us. She was only five and half years old, but she had shared those years with us and we were bereft when she died. Kissy and Holly always sat in the front seat of the van but after Holly died, Kissy would only lie under the back seat and whimper. I brought her to the vet who said there was nothing physically wrong with her. Like us, she was suffering from loss and grief.

Soon afterwards she accompanied us on a trip to Granada. We crossed a wide bridge and when we eventually reached the other side, Kissy looked back towards the van. We could see it in the distance but no one was near it, nor were there any people on the bridge. She raced eagerly back towards the van. We figured something was up and followed her. When we reached the van she was dancing around it. Her whole being radiated happiness and excitement. When we opened the van doors she jumped into the front seat and sat there, panting joyously. For that brief while, she was the old Kissy. Although I did not see anything, no sign or omen that Holly was present, I knew her spirit had rejoined us for a short while.

When we returned home from our holiday, we paid a visit to a pet shop to buy some supplies for Kissy and Cassy. We saw a little pup looking out at us through a cage. I tried to ignore her. After Holly's death, I didn't believe we could replace her with another dog. But Coco, as we would call her, had other intentions. She wanted to belong to us and her pleading eyes were so persuasive that, despite my firmest intentions, I walked from that pet shop with her in my arms. She came to us for a reason. Last year Cassy died with renal failure. She had shared our lives for sixteen and a half years and we found it impossible to imagine life without her. On the last night of her life, she went out to the garden to relieve herself. When she returned to the house she walked over to Coco who was sitting on the floor watching her. She rubbed Coco's nose. It was as if she was giving her a kiss or, maybe, passing on to her the responsibility of taking care of us. The next morning, Cassy had died. I'll never forget the tears were shed, not just by us but by all our neighbours who came to see her and who had also loved her.

Our three dogs, Holly, Kissy and Cassy, are buried together in Spain. Angel Ann has told me that our animals also enter their own realm of angels. Like us, they are carried over that bridge into their next life and welcomed into the world of spirit. Until we are reunited with them, they receive all the love and attention we lavished on them when they were our companions on earth.

Recently, I was contacted by a man whose pet dog had died. The man and dog had spent many years together and had a close and loving bond. The man was distraught when his dog became terminally ill and had to be put to sleep. He was with his dog to the very end and watched his eyes close and his breathing slow. Since then, he is convinced he can hear his dog barking. He is acutely familiar with the sound and knows he is not dreaming. I believe him.

I hope my answers have helped those of you who are opening up to the presence of your angels. Quite often, the questions I'm asked are of a more personal nature and are usually about the passing of a loved relation. However, there are some questions that stump even the most insightful angel. Like the woman who asked me to ask Angel Ann where her departed mother had pawned her fur coat. I listened in vain for Angel Ann's answer. I suspect she was too busy laughing to reply.

Epilogue

THE YEARNING TO UNDERSTAND THE GIFTS I have received remains strong. There is so much more I need to learn. This urge will not leave me until the day Angel Ann has told me that this is my last journey on earth. I will not return again. I am homeward bound but not, she assures me, for some time yet. I still have much to do before my life here is over.

I still search for memories of previous lives. Images surface but they are like shattered glass casting only fragmented impressions. I cannot peer through their mystery. But as this journey continues to unfold, the more I am convinced that I walked this path in another time. The voices of angels speak of a place where I once truly belonged and to where I will return.

This world of light holds everything for us. It is a world of endless beauty. A world that is totally real to all of us and yet sometimes we turn away, not knowing or trying to understand that this is our heritage. It is our source. It is the very place we originally came from. Its light carries us onwards to accomplish everything God has set down for us in this life. We must have faith in His wisdom. To acknowledge that He is a part of us and that we are emerging within Him.

Let us look inwards into our hearts and see the richness we carry within us. Let us stand tall before the love of God, who directs our way. We do not know what else our journey contains. But the bridge between our two worlds is like a stairway that we can climb each time we long to hear the voices of angels.

As I came to the conclusion of this book, a beautiful new light arrived into the world – my beautiful granddaughter Cara, born on 23 February 2011, weighing 8lb 10ozs. I thanked God and my beautiful angels who helped guide her into this world safely.

Thank you.

Show Me the Way, O Lord

Wrap your arms around them, Lord
and handle them with care.
Cast away all their doubts
and things that seem unfair.

Lay the pebbles on the ground
so they may walk ahead
and every time they take a step
you will stand in line ahead.
Show them, Lord, where they must go
to be one with you and I.
Every time they take a step
you are gently standing by.

Let them hear you whisper
the words that they must know.
Let them see the path ahead
To help them grow and grow.

Tell them, Lord, that you are one
with the universe and I
and all the healing that we have
is channelled from the sky.

Let them see the healing power
that lives inside of them
and every time you cast a doubt
you will pick them up again.

Let them hear the spirit guides
who walk with them today.
Let them see that shining light
that shines their very way.

So wrap your arms around them, Lord
and show them where to go.
For they are spirits of the light
and everyone must know.

By Angel Jonathan
Channelled by Francesca Brown

Grant Me An Angel

Grant me an angel
so I can see
the beautiful path
that you have set for me.

Show me an angel
in her splendid light
please let her guide me
to the place that is right.

If I don't see her
as she comes my way
please hold my hand
on this beautiful day.

In all of my heart
A love that is true
is the light from an angel.

A gift from you
As she comes closer
to show me the way
tell her I love her
and I welcome her
here today.

By Angel Jonathan

Channelled by Francesca Brown

Friends

There are many angels in our midst
some we'll love and some we'll kiss.
Angels are our greatest friends.
To know them is our gift.
They are here to bring great joy
to all God's creatures, young and small.
Angels are a gift from God.
They come to help us when we call.
Greet your angel and hear her sing
your name is carved upon her wing.
She has been with you on this earth.
That little friend who hails each birth.
She is the friend who walks with you.
That special friend you never knew.
But some day soon she'll whisper low
'I am you angel. Now you know.'